THE FOOL'S REVENGE
AND
LUCRETIA BORGIA

BY

VICTOR HUGO

WITH ILLUSTRATIONS

Fredonia Books
Amsterdam. The Netherlands

The Fool's Revenge and Lucretia Borgia:
Two Short Plays by Victor Hugo

by
Victor Hugo

ISBN: 1-58963-484-5

Copyright © 2001 by Fredonia Books

Fredonia Books
Amsterdam, The Netherlands
http://www.fredoniabooks.com

All rights reserved, including the right to reproduce this book, or portions thereof, in any form.

In order to make original editions of historical works available to scholars at an economical price, this facsimile of the original edition is reproduced from the best available copy and has been digitally enhanced to improve legibility, but the text remains unaltered to retain historical authenticity.

THE FOOL'S REVENGE

(LE ROI S'AMUSE.)

AS ADAPTED BY TOM TAYLOR.

DRAMATIS PERSONÆ.

BERTUCCIO, *the Duke's jester.*
GALEOTTO MANFREDI, *Lord of Faenza.*
GUIDO MALATESTA, *an old Condottiere.*
SERAFINO DELL' AQUILA, *poet and improvisatore*
BALDASSARE TORELLI, } *nobles.*
GIAN MARIA ORDELAFFI, }
BERNARDO ASCOLTI, *a Florentine envoy.*
ASCANIO, *a page.*
FRANCESCA BENTIVOGLIO, *wife of Manfredi.*
FIORDELISA, *daughter of Bertuccio.*
BRIGITTA, *Bertuccio's servant.*
GINEVRA, *wife of Malatesta.*

FAENZA. 1488.

THE FOOL'S REVENGE.

ACT I.

SCENE. — *The stage represents a loggia opening on the gardens of* MANFREDI'S *palace; a low terrace at the back, and beyond a view of the city and country adjacent. Moonlight. The gardens and loggia illuminated for a festa.*

SCENE I.

Nobles and Ladies discovered R. *and* C., *and moving through the gardens and loggia. Music at a distance.* TORELLI *and* ORDELAFFI *discovered. Enter* ASCOLTI, L.

TORELLI.

Messer Bernardo, you shall judge between us:
Is Ordelaffi's here, a feasting face?
I say, 't is fitter for a funeral.

ASCOLTI.

An Ordelaffi scarce can love the feast
That greets Octavian Riario,
Lord of Forli and Imola.

ORDELAFFI.

Because our line were masters there of old,
Till they were fools enough to get pulled down.
I was born to no lordship but my sword.
Thanks to my stout black bands, I look to win

New titles, and so grieve not over lost ones.
My glove upon 't! I 'll prove a lighter dancer,
A lustier wooer, and a deeper drinker
Than e'er a landed lordling of you all.
Is it a wager?
[GINEVRA *passes with* MANFREDI *from* L. *to* R. MALATESTA
appears L., *watching them.*

TORELLI.

My hand to that! There 's Malatesta's wife,
The fair Ginevra. Let 's try lucks with her.

ASCOLTI.

Ware hawk! Grey Guido 's an old-fashioned husband;
Look how he glares upon the Lord Manfredi.
Each of his soft words to the fair Ginevra 's
A dagger in the old fool's heart.

ORDELAFFI.

Sublime! Ripe sixty wedded to sixteen,
And thinks to shut the foxes from his grapes!

TORELLI.

The Duke, too, for his rival! Poor old man!

ASCOLTI.

Let the Duke look to it. Ginevra's smiles
May breed him worse foes than Count Malatesta.
[*Whispering.*] The Duchess!

TORELLI.

Faith! 't is ill rousing Bentivoglio blood.

ORDELAFFI.

And she 's as jealous as her own pet greyhound.

TORELLI.

And sharper in the teeth. I wonder much
She leaves Faenza, knowing her Manfredi
So general a lover.

ASCOLTI.

She leaves Faenza

TORELLI.

So they say, — to-morrow
Rides to Bologna to her grim old father,
Giovanni Bentivoglio.

ASCOLTI.

To complain
Of her hot-blooded husband?

TORELLI.

Nay, I know not;
Enough, she goes, and — fair dame as she is —
A murrain go with her, say I. There never
Was good time in Faenza, since *she* came
To spoil sport with her jealousy. Manfredi
Will be himself again when she is hence.

ASCOLTI.

Hush! here she comes —

ORDELAFFI.

With that misshapen imp.
Bertuccio. Gibing devil! I shall thrust
My dagger down his throat, one of these days!

TORELLI.

Call him a jester? He laughs vitriol!

ASCOLTI.

Spares nothing; cracks his random scurrile quips
Upon my master, great Lorenzo's self.

ORDELAFFI.

Do the knave justice; he's a king of tongue-fence.
Not a weak joint in all our armours round,
But he knows, and can hit. Confound the rogue!
I'm blistered still from a word-basting he
Gave me but yesterday. Would we were quits!

TORELLI.

Wait! I've a rod in pickle that shall flay
The tough hide off his hump. A rare revenge!

ASCOLTI.

They're here — avoid!
[ASCOLTI, ORDELAFFI, *and* TORELLI *retire up* C *and mingle with the guests. Enter* FRANCESCA *and* BERTUCCIO R., *followed by her two women.*

FRANCESCA (*looking off, as if watching, and to herself*).
Still with her! changing hot plans and long looks!
Hers for the dance, hers at the feast, — all hers!
Nothing for me but shallow courtesies,
And hollow coin of compliment that leaves
The craving heart as empty as a beggar
Bemocked with counters!

BERTUCCIO (*counting on his fingers and looking at the moon*).
Moon — Manfredi — moon!

FRANCESCA.

Ha, knave!

BERTUCCIO.

By your leave, Monna Cecca, I am ciphering.

FRANCESCA.

Some fool's sum?

BERTUCCIO.

                Yes, running your husband's changes
Against the moon's.   Manfredi has it hollow.
It comes out ten new loves 'gainst five new moons!

FRANCESCA.

Where do I stand?

BERTUCCIO.

First among the ten; your moon was a whole honey one.
Excluding that, it's nine loves to four moons.

FRANCESCA.

You pity me, Bertuccio?

BERTUCCIO.

                Not a whit.
I pity sparrows, but not sparrow-hawks.

FRANCESCA.

I read your riddle.   I am strong enough
To right my own wrongs!   So I am, while here.

BERTUCCIO.

Then stay!

FRANCESCA.

        My father, at Bologna, looks for me.

BERTUCCIO.

Then go!

FRANCESCA.

            And leave him here — with her — both free,
And not a friend that I can trust to watch
And give me due report how things go 'twixt them?
Had I one friend —

BERTUCCIO.
You have Bertuccio.

FRANCESCA.

Men call you faithless, bitter, loving wrong
For wrong's sake, Duke Manfredi's worst counsellor,
Still prompting him to evil.

BERTUCCIO.
How folks flatter!

FRANCESCA.

How, then, am I to trust you?

BERTUCCIO.
Monna Cecca,
You know the wild beasts that your husband keeps
Down in the castle fosse? There's a she-leopard
I lie and gaze at by the hour together;
So sleek, so graceful, and so dangerous!
I long to see her let loose on a man.
Trust me to draw the bolt, and loose *my* leopard.

FRANCESCA.

I'll trust your love of mischief — not of me.

BERTUCCIO.

That's safest!

FRANCESCA.
I must know how fares this fancy
Of Duke Manfredi for yon pale Ginevra.
Mark him and her, — their meetings, communings;
I know you're private with my lord.

BERTUCCIO (*with a dry chuckle*).
He trusts me!

FRANCESCA.

Here! take my ring; your letters sealed with this,
My page Ascanio will bring me straight.
T is but three hours' hard riding, and in six
I 'm here again. Mark! write not on suspicion.
Let evil thought ripen to evil act,
That in the full flush of their guilty joys
I may strike sudden and strike home.
No Bentivoglio pardons.

BERTUCCIO.
Have a care!
Faenza is Manfredi's! These court-flies,
[*Pointing to the guests.*
Who flutter in the sunshine of his favour,
Have stings; the pudding-headed citizens
Love his free ways, — he leaves *their* wives alone.
You play your own head, touching *his*.

FRANCESCA.

Give me my vengeance, — then come what come may.
Enough! I am resolved. Now for the dance!
They shall not see a cloud upon my brow,
Though my heart ache and burn. I can smile, too,
On him and her. Bertuccio, remember!
[*Exit* FRANCESCA, *followed by her women*, R.

BERTUCCIO (*looking at the ring*).
A blood-stone — apt reminder!
Does she think
That none but her have wrongs? That none but her
Means to revenge them? What! "No Bentivoglio
Pardons?" There is a certain vile Bertuccio.

A twisted, withered, hunch-backed court buffoon, —
A thing to make mirth, and to be made mirth of;
A something betwixt ape and man, — that claims
To run in couples with your ladyship.
You hunt Manfredi; I hunt Malatesta.
Let's try which of the two has sharper fangs!

[MANFREDI *and* GINEVRA *appear in the background*, R.
The Duke and Malatesta's wife! [*He retires up stage.*
[MANFREDI *and* GINEVRA *come forward;* MALATESTA
watching them, L.

MANFREDI.

Not yet, — but one more round! The feast is blank
For me when you are gone. The flowers lack perfume,
Missing your fragrant breath. The music sounds
Harsh and untunable when your sweet voice
Makes no more under melody. Oh, stay!

GINEVRA.

I am summoned, sir; my husband waits for me.

MANFREDI.

What spoil-sports are these husbands! [*Aside.*] And these wives
Per Bacco! I could wish Count Malatesta
Would lend my duchess escort to Bologna,
So we were both well rid. [MALATESTA *beckons to* GINEVRA.

GINEVRA.

     Your pardon, sir.
My husband beckons. It is I, not you,
Must bear his moods to-night; I dare not stay.

MANFREDI.

I would not bring a cloud to your fair brow
For all Faenza. Fare you well, sweet lady!
      [*He leads her to* MALATESTA.

I render up your jewel, Malatesta;
See that you guard it as befits its price.

MALATESTA.
Trust me for that, my lord.

MANFREDI (*to* GENEVRA).
　　　　　　Sweet dreams wait on you.

MALATESTA (*aside*).
This night sees *her* safe past Faenza's walls;
She's too fair for this liquorish court of ours.
　　　　　[*Exeunt* MALATESTA *and* GINEVRA, L.

MANFREDI.
A peerless lady!

BERTUCCIO (*coming forward*).
　　　　　And a churlish spouse!

MANFREDI.
Bertuccio!

BERTUCCIO.
"At your elbow, sir!" quoth Satanus.

MANFREDI.
Come, fool, let's rail at husbands.

BERTUCCIO.
　　　　　Shall I call
Your wife to help us?

MANFREDI.
　　　　　Out on thee, screech-owl!
Just when I felt my chains about to fall
Thou mind'st me of my jailer. Thank the saints,
I shall be free to-morrow, for a while

I'm thirsty to employ my liberty.
Come, my familiar, help me to some mischief, —
Some pleasant deviltry, with just the spice
Of sin to make the enjoyment exquisite.

BERTUCCIO.

Let's see! Throat-cutting's pleasant, but that's stale;
Plotting has savour in it, but 't is too tedious;
Say, a campaign with Ordelaffi's band,
So you may feed all the seven sins at once?

MANFREDI.

Out, barren hound! thy wits are growing dull.

BERTUCCIO.

A man can't always be finding out new sins, —
Think they 're as hard to hit on as new pleasures.
My head on 't, Alexander had not run
So wide a round of pleasures as you of sins,
And yet he offered kingdoms for a new one.
You must invoke Asmodeus, not Beelzebub.

MANFREDI.

What's he?

BERTUCCIO.

The devil specially charged with love;
He has more work to do than all the infernal legion.
There's Malatesta's wife; she's young and fair,
And good, they say. Rare matter for *sin* there,
Though 't is the oldest of them all.

MANFREDI.

But show me
How to win *her!* She's cold as she is fair;
I have spent enough sweet speech to have softened stone
And all in vain.

BERTUCCIO.

                The monks say Hannibal
Melted the rocks with vinegar, not sugar.

MANFREDI.

But she is adamant!

BERTUCCIO.

                    When all else fails,
You've still force to fall back on. Carry her off
From under Guido's grizzled beard.

MANFREDI.

                            By Bacchus,
There's metal in thy counsel, knave! I'll think on 't.

BERTUCCIO.

It needs no brains neither, — only strong hands
And hard hearts. Here come both.
           [*Enter* TORELLI, ASCOLTI, *and* ORDELAFFI, C.

MANFREDI.

What say you, gentlemen; may I trust your arms?

TORELLI.

They're yours in any quarrel.

ASCOLTI.

                So are mine!

ORDELAFFI.

                          And mine!

BERTUCCIO.

One at a time. You said "*arms!*" Of Torelli
You should ask *legs!* His did such famous service
In carrying him out of danger at Sarzana,
I think they may be trusted. [*All laugh except* TORELLI

TORELLI.

      Scurrile knave!
But I'll be even with thee!

BERTUCCIO.

      That were pity.
A hump would be a sore disfigurement
Upon a back that you're so fond of showing!

ASCOLTI.

This rogue needs gagging.

BERTUCCIO (*to* ASCOLTI).

      What, for speaking truth?
I cry you mercy! I forgot how ugly
It must sound to a Florentine Ambassador —

MANFREDI.

Well thrust, Bertuccio!

ORDELAFFI (*angrily*).

      My lord! my lord!
The slave is paid to find us *wit* —

BERTUCCIO (*interrupting*).

      Hold there!
No man is bound to impossibilities, —
'T is a known maxim of the Roman law;
How then can I find wit for Ordelaffi?
      [*All laugh but* ORDELAFFI
But look! there's Serafino, big with a sonnet:
I must help him to reason for his rhymes.

MANFREDI.

Stay!

BERTUCCIO.

Not I! You're for finding out new sins:
With three such counsellors, I am superfluous.
[*Aside.*] The evil seed is sown; 't will grow! 't will
    grow!   [*Exit* BERTUCCIO.

TORELLI.

Toad!

ASCOLTI.

Foul-mouthed scoffer!

ORDELAFFI.

                      Warped in wit and limb!

ASCOLTI.

My lord, you give your monkey too much rope.
He'll soon forget all tricks in the scurvy one
Of making his grinders meet in our soft parts.

MANFREDI.

Nay, give the devil his due; if he hits hard,
He hits impartially. I take my share
Of buffets with the rest. Best cure the smart
By laughing at your neighbour that smarts worse;
But about this business, where *your* arms may help me.

ASCOLTI.

Is it an enemy to be silenced?

ORDELAFFI.

                A castle
To be surprised? A merchant to be squeezed?

ASCOLTI.

Or aught in which ducats or brains of Florence
Can help?

MANFREDI.

No. Who was queen of the feast to-night
In your skilled judgment, Messer Gian Maria?

ORDELAFFI.

I ought to say your duchess, fair Francesca;
But if another tongue had asked the question —

MANFREDI.

Speak out thy honest judgment!

ORDELAFFI.

Not a lady
In all Faenza's worthy to compare
With proud Ginevra Malatesta!

TORELLI.

I think I know a fairer — but no matter!

MANFREDI.

I hold with Ordelaffi. I have mounted
Ginevra's colours in my cap and heart;
But she's too proud, or fearful of old Guido,
To smile upon my suit. 'T is the first time
I've found so coy a dame.

ASCOLTI.

Trust one who knows them
The coyest are not always chastest.

MANFREDI.

How say you, if I spared her shame of yielding
By a night escalade?

ORDELAFFI (*shaking his head*)
        Carry her off?
A Malatesta! Were it an enemy's town —

MANFREDI.

Hear him! How modestly he talks! Why, man,
Since when shrank'st thou from climbing balconies,
And forcing doors without an invitation?

ORDELAFFI.

Oh, citizens, I grant you; but a noble's!
One of ourselves!

ASCOLTI.
        Remember, Malatesta
Is cousin to the old lord of Cesena.
The affair might breed a feud, and so let in
The sly Venetian.

TORELLI.
        Be advised, my lord;
If you must breathe your new-fledged liberty,
Try safer game! Old Malatesta's horns
Might prove too sharp for pastime!

MANFREDI.
                Out, you faint hearts!
Do you fall off? Then, by St. Francis' bones,
I and Bertuccio will adventure it.

TORELLI.

Bertuccio! My jewel to his hump,
T was he put this mad frolic in your head!

MANFREDI.

And if it were? At least he'll stand by me.
Perchance his wits may be worth all your brawn.

ASCOLTI.

Here comes one who may claim to be consulted
Upon this business.   [*Enter* MALATESTA, L.

MANFREDI (*disconcerted*).

                    Guido Malatesta!
Why, how now, Count? You left our feast so soon,
I thought you warm i' the sheets this good half hour.

MALATESTA.

I had forgot my duty to your lordship,
So now repair my lack of courtesy.
To-morrow I purpose riding to Cesena,
And would not go without due leave-taking.

MANFREDI (*aside*).

This jumps well with my project.
[*Aloud.*] What, to-morrow!
You ride alone?

MALATESTA.

            No, with my wife.

MANFREDI (*aside*).

                        The devil!
[*Aloud.*] Why, this is sudden. She spoke no word of this
To-night.

MALATESTA.

      Tush! Women know not their own minds,
How should they know their husband's?

MANFREDI.

                        But your reason?

MALATESTA.

Your air here in Faenza is too warm,
And scarce so pure as fits my wife's complexion.

She'll be better in my castle at Cesena;
The walls are five feet thick, and from the platform
There's a rare view. She'll need no exercise.

MANFREDI (*aside*).
The jailer! [*Aloud.*] But what says the lady's will?

MALATESTA.
I never ask that, and so escape all risk
Of finding it run counter to my own.

MANFREDI.
Faenza will have great miss of you both.

MALATESTA.
Oh, fear not; I'll return. Your wine's too good
To be left lightly. I'll be back to-morrow,
Before the gates are shut. Meanwhile, accept
This leave-taking by proxy from my wife.

MANFREDI.
Not so; I must exchange farewell with her
To-morrow.

MALATESTA.
   We shall start an hour ere dawn;
You'll scarce be stirring.

MANFREDI (*aside*).
     Plague upon the churl!
He meets me at all points. [*Aloud.*] At least, I hope
This absence of your wife will not be long;
My duchess cannot spare her. [*Aside.*] Saints forgive me!

MALATESTA.

When your fair lady wants her, she can send:
I'll answer for her coming on *that* summons.
Good-night, sweet lords. [*Aside.*] How crestfallen he
  looks!
Mass! 't is ill cozening an old condottiere!
Did he think I had forgot to guard my baggage? [*Exit.*

MANFREDI.

A murrain go with him! May the horse stumble
That carries him, and break his old bull-neck!
Oh, this is cruel! with my hand stretched out,
To have to draw 't back empty. I could curse!

TORELLI.

What if I helped you to a substitute
For coy Ginevra, passing her in beauty?
One, too, whose conquest puts no crown to risk,
And helps withal a notable requital
That we all owe Bertuccio, you included.

MANFREDI.

What mean you?

TORELLI.

Guess what's happened to Bertuccio.

ORDELAFFI.

He's grown good-natured?

ASCOLTI.

Or has dropped his hump?

MANFREDI.

He has found a monkey uglier than himself?

TORELLI.
No, something stranger than all these would be,
If they *had* happened, — he has found a mistress!
[*All burst out laughing.*

MANFREDI.
My lady's pet baboon? Bertuccio
Graced with a mistress? [*He laughs.*

ASCOLTI.
She is blind, of course?

ORDELAFFI.
And has a hump, I hope, to match his own?
What a rare breed 't will be, of two-humped babes,
Like Bactrian camels!

MANFREDI.
Bertuccio with a mistress! Why, the rogue
Ne'er yet made joke so monstrous or so pleasant!
[*They laugh again.*

TORELLI.
Laugh as you please, sirs; on my knightly faith,
He *has* a mistress, — and a rare one, too!
Nay, if you doubt my word — Here comes Dell' Aquila;
He knows, as well as I.

MANFREDI.
We'll question him.
[*Enter* SERAFINO DELL' AQUILA, C.
Good-even to my poet. You walk late.

DELL' AQUILA (*pointing to the moon*).
I tend my mistress: poets and lunatics,
You know, are her liege subjects.

MANFREDI.
                    They are happy!

DELL' AQUILA.
Why?

MANFREDI.
    They have a new mistress every month,
And each month's mistress no two nights alike.
But jesters can find mistresses, it seems,
As well as poets.   There's Torelli swears
Bertuccio has one, and that you know it.

DELL' AQUILA.
I know he has a rare maid close mewed up,
But whether wife or daughter —

MANFREDI.
                    Tell not me!
A mistress for a thousand!   But what of her?
How did you find her out?

DELL' AQUILA.
                    'T was some weeks since
Attending vespers in your house's chapel,
At San Costanza, I beheld a maiden
Kneeling before that picture of Our Lady
By Fra Filippo, — oh, so fair, so rapt
In her pure, passionate prayers!   I tell you, sirs,
I was nigh going on my knees beside her,
And asking for an interest in her orisons:
Such eyes of softest blue, crowned with such wreaths
Of glossy chestnut hair; a cheek of snow
Plushed tenderly, as when the sunlight strikes
Upon an evening alp; and over all,
A grace of maiden modesty that lay

More still and snowy round her than the folds
Of her white veil. And when she rose, I rose
And followed her, like one drawn by a charm,
To a mean house, where entering, she was lost.

MANFREDI.

She was alone?

DELL' AQUILA.

Only a shrewish servant
That saw her to the church, and saw her home.

MANFREDI.

A most weak wolf-dog for so choice a lamb!

DELL' AQUILA.

Methought, my lord, she needed no more guard
Than the innocence that sat, dove-like, in her eyes,
That shaped the folding of her delicate hands,
And timed the movement of her gentle feet.

MANFREDI.

You spoke to her?

DELL' AQUILA.

I dared not; some strange shame
Put weight upon my tongue. I only watched her,
And sometimes heard her sing. That was enough.

MANFREDI.

Poets are easy satisfied. Well, you watched?

DELL' AQUILA.

And then I found that I was not alone
Upon my nightly post: there were two more;
One stayed outside, like me, and one went in.

TORELLI.

True to the letter! I was the outsider;
The third, and luckiest, was Bertuccio!

MANFREDI.

The hump-backed hypocrite!

ORDELAFFI.

The owl that screeched
The loudest against women!

ASCOLTI.

But is 't certain
That 't was Bertuccio?

TORELLI.

I can swear to that!

DELL' AQUILA.

And I!

ASCOLTI.

How do you know him?

TORELLI.

By his hump,
His gait — who could mistake that crab-like walk?
I could have knocked my head against the wall
To think I had been fool enough to trust
A woman's looks for once. Dell' Aquila,
I know, holds other faith about the sex.

DELL' AQUILA.

I would stake life upon her purity;
Yet, 't is past doubt Bertuccio is the man,
The ugly jailer of this prisoned bird.

MANFREDI.

Why, that's enough to make it a mere duty
To break her prison-house, and shift her keeping
To fitter hands, — say, mine. I'm lord of the town;
None else has right of prison here, but me.

DELL' AQUILA.

What would you do?

MANFREDI.

      First see if she bears out
Your picture, Serafino; if she do,
Be sure I will not wait outside to mark
Her shadow. Shadows may suit poets; I
Want substance.

TORELLI.

     She's meat for Bertuccio's master,
Not for Bertuccio. When shall it be?

MANFREDI.

         To-morrow
I'm a free man! Meet me at midnight, here.

DELL' AQUILA.

You would not harm her? Only see her face;
You will not have the heart to do her wrong.

MANFREDI.

What call you "wrong"? — to save so choice a creature
From such a guardian as Bertuccio?
He would have prompted me to play the robber
Of Malatesta's pearl. Let him guard his own!

ORDELAFFI.

If he resists, we'll knock him over the sconce;
Let me have *that* part of the business.

MANFREDI.

Nay, I'd not have the rascal harmed; he's bitter,
But shrewdly witty, and he makes me laugh.
No, spare me my buffoon; who does him harm,
Shall answer it to me.

TORELLI.

'T were a rare plot to make the knave believe
Our scheme still held against old Malatesta, —
That his Ginevra was the game we followed.

ORDELAFFI.

So give him a rendezvous a mile away;
And while he waits our coming, to break open
The mew where he keeps close his tassel-gentle.

ASCOLTI (*aside to* MANFREDI).

Ne'er trust a poet. What if he betrayed us?

MANFREDI.

He's truth itself; and where he gives his faith,
'T is better than a bond of your Lorenzo's.

ASCOLTI.

Swear him to secrecy.

MANFREDI (*to* DELL' AQUILA).

           Your hand upon it:
You'll not spoil our sport by breaking to Bertuccio
What we intend?

DELL' AQUILA.

           But think, oh, think, my lord,
What if this were no mistress — as — if looks
Have privilege to reveal the soul — she is none!

MANFREDI.

Mistress or maid, man, I will not be balked;
'T is for her good. I know the sex; she pines
In her captivity. I'll find a cage
More fitting such a bird as you've described.
Your hand on't: not a whisper to Bertuccio!

DELL' AQUILA.

You force me! There's my hand! I will not speak
A word to him!

MANFREDI (*taking his hand*).
           That's like a trusty liegeman
Of blind Lord Cupid!—Hark! a word with you.
           [MANFREDI *and Lords talk apart*, C.

DELL' AQUILA.

I'll save her from this wrong, or lose myself.
What tie there is betwixt these two, I know not,—
How one so fair and seeming gentle's linked
With one so foul and bitter, a buffoon,
Who makes *his* vile office viler still
By prompting to the evil that he mocks.
But I will 'gage my life that she is pure,
And still shall be so, if my aid avail!
           [MANFREDI *and Lords separate.*
Once more, my lord: you'll not be stayed from this
That you propose?

MANFREDI.

           Unconscionable bard!
What! when you've set my mouth a-watering
You'd have me put the dainty morsel from me?
Go, feed on signs and shadows! Such thin stuff
Is the best diet for you singing birds;
We eagles must have flesh!

DELL' AQUILA (*to all*).

                            Good-night, my lords!
[*Aside.*] Keep to your carrion, kites! She's not for *you*.
                                  [*Exit* DELL' AQUILA.

MANFREDI.

But how to get sight of Bertuccio's jewel!
I'd see, before I'd snatch.

TORELLI.

                      Trust me for that.
I am no poet. When I found the damsel
Admitted such a gallant as Bertuccio,
I thought it time to press my suit, and so
Accosted her on her way from San Costanza —

MANFREDI.

She listened?

TORELLI.

                Long enough — the little fool! —
To learn my meaning, then she flushed and fled;
I followed — when, as the foul fiend would have it,
Ginevra Malatesta coming by
From vespers, with her train, sheltered the pigeon,
And spoiled my chase.

MANFREDI.

                   You did not give it up?

TORELLI.

I changed my plan; the mistress being coy,
I spread my net to catch the maid, — oh, lord!
The veriest Gorgon! You might swear none e'er
Had given *her* chase before; no coyness there.
A small expense of oaths and coin sufficed
To make her think herself a misprized Venus,

And me the most discriminating wooer
In all Faenza. 'T will not need much art
For me to win an entrance to the house;
And when I'm in it, it shall go hard, my lord,
But I find means to get you access too.

MANFREDI.

About it straight; at dusk to-morrow night
Be here, armed, masked, and cloaked.

ORDELAFFI.

                         While poor Bertuccio
Awaits our coming near San Stefano, —
A stone's throw from the casa Malatesta.

ASCOLTI.

He's here!   [*Enter* BERTUCCIO, L.

BERTUCCIO.

        Not yet a-bed!
Since when were the fiend's eggs so hard to hatch?
I left a pleasant little germ of sin
Some half an hour since; it should be full-grown
By this time. Is it?

MANFREDI.

                Winged and hoofed and tailed.
If proud Ginevra Malatesta sleep
To-morrow night beneath old Guido's roof,
Then call me a snow-water-blooded shaveling.

BERTUCCIO.

Ha! 'T is resolved then?

TORELLI.

                   We have pledged our faith
To carry off the fairest in Faenza —

THE FOOL'S REVENGE.

ASCOLTI.

Before the stroke of midnight.

ORDELAFFI.

'T was my plan
To gather one by one to the place of action;
Lest, going in a troop, we might awake
Suspicion, and put Guido on his guard.

BERTUCCIO.

A wise precaution, although it *was* yours.
I wronged you, gentlemen; I thought you shrunk
Even from sin, when there was danger in 't.
It seems there *are* deeds black enough to make
Even Torelli brave, Ascolti prompt,
And Ordelaffi witty.   But the place?

MANFREDI.

Beside San Stefano.

BERTUCCIO.

The hour of meeting?

MANFREDI.

Half an hour after vespers.   There await us.
And now good rest, my lords; the night wanes fast
My duchess will be weary.

ALL (*going*).

Sir, good-night!

BERTUCCIO.

Sleep well, Torelli.   Dream of charging home
In the van of some fierce fight.

TORELLI.
My common dream.

BERTUCCIO.
'T is natural, — dreams go by contraries.
And you, Ascolti, dream of telling truth;
And, Ordelaffi, that you 've grown wise.

TORELLI.
And you, that your back 's straight, your legs a match.

ASCOLTI.
And your tongue tipped with honey.

ORDELAFFI.
Come, my lords;
Leave him to spit his venom at the moon,
As they say toads do!

BERTUCCIO.
Take my curse among you,
Fair, false, big, brainless, outside shows of men;
For once your gibes and jeers fall pointless from me.
My great revenge is nigh, and drowns all sense,
I am straight and fair and well-shaped as yourselves;
Vengeance swells out my veins, and lifts my head,
And makes me terrible! Come, sweet to-morrow,
And put my enemy's heart into my hand
That I may gnaw it!

ACT II.

SCENE.— *A room in the house of* BERTUCCIO, *hung with tapestry; a coloured statue of the Madonna in a recess, with a small lamp burning before it; carved and coloured furniture; a carved cabinet and large carved coffers; in the centre a window opening on the street, with a balcony; behind the tapestry, a secret door communicating with the street,* L. 2 E.; *a door,* R. 2 E.; *a lamp lighted; a lute and flowers; a missal on a stand before the statue, a recess concealed by the tapestry,* L. 3 E.

SCENE I.

TORELLI *and* BRIGITTA *discovered,* C.

BRIGITTA.

Hark, there's the quarter. You must hence, fair signor.

TORELLI.

But a few moments more of your sweet presence!

BRIGITTA.

Saint Ursula, she knows, 't is not my will
That drives you hence; but if my master found
That I received a man into the house,
'T were pity of my place, if not my life.

TORELLI.

Your master is a churl, that would condemn
These maiden blooms to wither on the tree.

BRIGITTA.

Churl you may call him! Why, he'd have the house
A prison. If you heard the coil he keeps

Of bolts and bars and locks! Lord knows the twitter
I've been in all to-day about the key
I lost this morning; it unlocks the door
Of the turnpike stair that leads down to the street.

TORELLI.

'T was lucky I came by just when you dropped it.

BRIGITTA.

Dropped! — nay, signor, 't was whipped off by some cut-purse
That thought to filch my coin.

TORELLI.
      That's a shrewd guess!
He must have flung it from him where I found it,
Not knowing [*bowing to her*] of what jewel it unlocked
 the casket!

BRIGITTA.

How can I ever pay your pains that brought it back?

TORELLI.

By ever and anon giving me leave
To come and sun myself in your chaste presence.

BRIGITTA (*coquettishly*).
Alas, sweet signor!

TORELLI (*in the same tone*).
    Oh, divine Brigitta!

BRIGITTA.

But I must say farewell. Vespers are over;
My mistress will be waiting; she's so fearful.

TORELLI.

As if her unripe beauties were in danger,
While your maturer loveliness can walk
The streets unguarded.

BRIGITTA.

Nay, I'm a poor, fond thing; Lord knows the risk
I run to let you in.

TORELLI.

I warrant now
You've some snug nook where, if your master came,
You could bestow me at a pinch.

BRIGITTA.

I know none,
Unless 't were here [*lifting arras* L. 3 E.] behind the arras
 look!
Here's a hole, too, whence you could peep to see
When the coast's clear.

TORELLI (*aside*).

There's room enough for two.
[*Sternly.*] Brigitta!

BRIGITTA.

Signor!

TORELLI (*with feigned suspicion*).

How if this had served
For hiding others before me?

BRIGITTA.

I swear
By the eleven thousand virgins —

TORELLI.
                That's
Too many by ten thousand and ten hundred
And ninety-nine! Vouch but your virgin self,
And I am satisfied.

BRIGITTA (*whimpering*).
            Alack-a-day!
To be suspected after all these years.

TORELLI.

Pardon a lover's jealousy; this kiss
Shall wipe away the memory of my wrong.
[*Aside.*] What will not loyalty drive a man to?
                            [*Kisses her.*
There!
BRIGITTA (*aside*).
        He has the sweetest lips! And now begone,
Sweet signor, if you love me.

TORELLI.
            If, Brigitta!
Banish me then to outer darkness straight!
Farewell, my full-blown rose — let others prize
The opening bud — the ripe, rich flower for me'

BRIGITTA.

Oh, the saints, how he talks! This way, sweet signor,
                [*Taking a key from her girdle.*
The secret door; the key you found and brought me
Unlocks it.   [*Unlocking secret door,* L. 2 E.

TORELLI (*taking another from his girdle, aside*).
        Else, why did I filch it from you —
And have this, its twin brother, forged to-day!
VOL. XIV. — 3

BRIGITTA (*getting the lamp*).
I'll light you out, and lock the door behind you,
"Safe bind, safe find."

TORELLI.

Good-night, sweet piece of woman,
I leave my heart in pledge. [*Aside.*] Now for the Duke.
[BRIGITTA *holds open the door and lights him down, then locks it.*

BRIGITTA.

He's gone, bless his sweet face! To think what risks
Men will run that are lovers, and indeed
Weak women, too! Lord! if my master knew.
[*Getting on her mantle.*
'T is lucky San Costanza is hard by,
I should be fearful else. Faenza's full
Of gallants, and who knows what might befall
A poor young woman like myself, with naught
Except her innocence to be her safeguard! [*Exit*, R. 2 E
[*As soon as she has closed the door, the secret door,* C., *opens and* TORELLI *re-appears.*

TORELLI.

This way, my lord; the dragon has departed.
[*Enter* MANFREDI *from the secret door*, L. 2 E

MANFREDI.
'T is time, I was weary of my watch.

TORELLI.

You were alone, at least. Think of *my* lot,
That had to make love to a tough old spinster.
I would we had changed parts. Why, good my lord,
I had to kiss her. Faugh! When shall I get

The garlic from my beard? But here's the cage
That holds our bird. We must ensconce ourselves,
For they'll be here anon; vespers were over
Before we entered.

MANFREDI.

Thanks to your device
Of the forged key. Yet that was scarcely needed;
I've climbed more break-neck balconies than that
[*Pointing to window.*
Without a silken ladder! [*Looking about.*] So — a lute —
A missal — flowers! — more tokens of a maid
Than of a mistress! Well, so much the better;
I long to see the girl. Is she as fair
As Serafino painted?

TORELLI.

Faith, my lord,
She's fair enough to justify more sonnets
Than e'er fat Petrarch pumped out for his Laura.
She is a paragon of blushing girlhood,
Full of temptation to the finger-tips.
I marvel at myself, that e'er I yielded
This amorous enterprise, even to you —
But that my loyalty outbears my love.

MANFREDI.

I will requite your loyalty; fear not;
But where shall we bestow ourselves?

TORELLI (*lifting the arras from the recess*).

In here;
The old crone showed it me but now there's cover
And peeping-place sufficient. Hark! they come!
Stand close, my lord.
[*They retire behind the arras. Enter* FIORDELISA *and*
BRIGITTA. R. 2 E

BRIGITTA.
And he was there to-night?

FIORDELISA.
Oh, yes! He offered me the holy water
As I passed in. I trembled so, Brigitta,
When our hands met, I fear he must have marked it,
But that he seemed almost as trembling, too,
As I was.

BRIGITTA.
He! a brazen popinjay,
I 'll warrant me, for all his downcast looks!
I wonder how my master would endure
To hear of such audacious goings on!

FIORDELISA.
That makes me sad. My father is so kind,
I cannot bear to have a secret from him.
Sometimes I feel as I would tell him all;
But then, I think, perhaps he would forbid me
From going out to church; and 't is so dull
To be shut up here all the long bright day:
From morn till dark, to mark the busy stir
Under the window, and the happy voices
Of holiday-makers, that go out and in
Just as they please. Look at the birds, Brigitta!
Their wings are free, yet no harm comes to them;
I'm sure *they're* innocent! And then to hear
Sometimes the trumpets, as the knights ride by,
And tramp of armed men; [*Lute sounds without.*] sometimes a lute.
Hark! 't is his lute! I know the air, how sweet!
My good Brigitta, would there be much harm
If I touched mine, only a little touch,
To tell him I am listening?

BRIGITTA.
Holy saints,
Was e'er such boldness! I must have your lute
Locked up. These girls! these girls! Bar them from
 Court,
And they'll find matter in church; keep them from
 speech,
And they'll make cat-gut do the work of tongue.
Better be charged to keep a cat from cream,
Than a girl from gallants!

FIORDELISA.
Nay but, good Brigitta,
This gentleman is none.

BRIGITTA.
How do *you* know?

FIORDELISA.
He never speaks to me, scarce looks, or if
He do, it is but to withdraw his gaze
As hastily as I do mine. I've seen him
Blush when our eyes met; not like yon rude man
Who pressed upon me with such words and looks
As made me red and hot; you know the time
When that kind lady, Countess Malatesta,
Scarce saved me from his boldness.

BRIGITTA.
Tilly-vally.
There are more ways of bird-catching than one;
He's the best fowler who least scares his quarry.
But I must go and see the supper toward.
Your father will be here anon! [*Exit* BRIGITTA, R.

FIORDELISA.
Dear father!
Would he were here that I might rest my head
Upon his breast, and have his arms about me;
For then I feel there's something I may love
And not be chidden for it. [*Lute sounds.*] Hark! again.
If I durst answer!
How sad he must be out there in the dark,
Not knowing if I mark his music.
[*Takes her lute, then puts it away.*
No!
My father would be angry; sad enough,
To have one joy I may not share with him;
Yet there can be no harm in listening.
I thought to-night he would have spoken to me,
But then Brigitta came, and he fell back!
I'm glad he did not speak, and yet I'm sorry,
I should so like to hear his voice, just once.
He comes in my dreams, now, but he never speaks.
I'm sure 't is soft and sweet! [*Listening.*] His lute is
  hushed.
What if I touch mine, now that he is gone?
I must not look out of the casement! Yes,
I'm sure he's gone?
[*Takes her lute and strikes a chord*, L.

MANFREDI (*aside, lifting the arras*).
She is worth ten Ginevras!

TORELLI (*holding him back*).
Not yet!

MANFREDI.
Unhand me, I *will* speak to her!
[BERTUCCIO *appears at the door*, R. 2 E.

TORELLI.

My lord! It is Bertuccio! In — quick!
[BERTUCCIO *stands for a moment fondly contemplating*
FIORDELISA; *his dress is sober and his manner composed. He steps quietly forward.*

BERTUCCIO.

My own!

FIORDELISA (*turning suddenly, and flinging herself into
his arms with a cry of joy*).
My father!

BERTUCCIO (*embracing her tenderly*).
Closer, closer yet!
Let me feel those soft arms about my neck,
This dear cheek on my heart! No, do not stir,
It does me so much good! I am so happy, —
These minutes are worth years!

FIORDELISA.
My own dear father!

BERTUCCIO.

Let me look at thee, darling. Why, thou growest
More and more beautiful! Thou 'rt happy here?
Hast all that thou desirest, — thy lute, thy flowers?
She loves her poor old father? Blessings on thee,
I know thou dost, but tell me so.

FIORDELISA.
I love you —
I love you very much! I am so happy
When you are with me. Why do you come so late,
And go so soon? Why not stay always here?

BERTUCCIO.

Why not! Why not! Oh, if I could! To live
Where there's no mocking, and no being mocked;
No laughter but what's innocent; no mirth
That leaves an after bitterness like gall.

FIORDELISA.

Now, you are sad! There's that black ugly cloud
Upon your brow; you promised, the last time,
It never *should* come when we were together.
You know when *you're* sad *I'm* sad too.

BERTUCCIO.

My bird!
I'm selfish even with thee; let dark thoughts come,
That thy sweet voice may chase them, as they say
The blessed church bells drive the demons off.

FIORDELISA.

If I but knew the reason of your sadness,
Then I might comfort you; but I know nothing,
Not even your name.

BERTUCCIO.

I'd have no name for thee
But "father."

FIORDELISA.

In the convent at Cesena,
Where I was reared, they used to call me orphan.
I thought I had no father, till you came,
And then they needed not to say I had one·
My own heart told me that.

BERTUCCIO.

I often think
I had done well to have left thee there, in the peace

Of that still cloister. But it was too hard;
My empty heart so hungered for my child!
For those dear eyes that look no scorn for me,
That voice that speaks respect and tenderness,
Even for me! My dove, my lily-flower,
My only stay in life. Oh, God! I thank thee
Thou hast left me this at least! [*He weeps.*

FIORDELISA.
                    Dear father!
You're crying now; you must not cry,— you must not.
I cannot bear to see you cry.

BERTUCCIO.
                    Let be!
'T were better than to see me laugh.

FIORDELISA.
                    But wherefore?
You say you are so happy here, and yet
You never come but to weep bitter tears.
And I can but weep too, not knowing why.
Why are you sad? Oh, tell me,— tell me all!

BERTUCCIO.

I cannot. In this house I am thy father;
Out of it, what I am boots not to say;
Hated, perhaps, or envied; feared, I hope,
By many; scorned by more; and loved by none.
In this one innocent corner of the world
I would but be to thee a father,— something
August and sacred!

FIORDELISA.
        And you are so, father.

BERTUCCIO.

I love thee with a love strong as the hate
I bear for all but thee.   Come, sit beside me,
With thy pure hand in mine, and tell me still,
"I love you," and " I love you," — only that.
Smile on me — so! thy smile is passing sweet!
Thy mother used to smile so once; oh, God!
I cannot bear it.   Do not smile; it wakes
Memories that tear my heart-strings.   Do not look
So like thy mother, or I shall go mad!

FIORDELISA.

Oh, tell me of my mother!

BERTUCCIO (*shuddering*).
No, no, no!

FIORDELISA.

She 's dead?

BERTUCCIO.
Yes.

FIORDELISA.
You were with her when she died?

BERTUCCIO.

No!   Leave the dead alone; talk of thyself,
Thy life here.   Thou heed'st well my caution, girl, —
Not to go out by day, nor show thyself
There, at the casement.

FIORDELISA.
Yes: some day, I hope,
You will take me with you, but to see the town;
'T is so hard to be shut up here, alone.

BERTUCCIO.

Thou hast *not* stirred abroad? [*Suspiciously and eagerly*.

FIORDELISA.

                Only to vespers;
You said I might do that with good Brigitta
I never go forth or come in alone.

BERTUCCIO.

That's well. I grieve that thou should'st live so close,
But if thou knewest what poison's in the air,
What evil walks the streets, how innocence
Is a temptation, beauty but a bait
For desperate desires — No man, I hope,
Has spoken to thee?

FIORDELISA.

Only one.

BERTUCCIO (*fiercely*).

Ha! who?

FIORDELISA.

I know not. 'T was against my will.

BERTUCCIO (*eagerly*).

                You gave
No answer

FIORDELISA.

No, I fled.

BERTUCCIO (*in the same tone*).

He followed you?

FIORDELISA.

A gracious lady gave me kind protection,
And bade her train guard me safe home. Oh, father,

If you had seen how good she was, how gently
She soothed my fears, — for I was sore afraid, —
I'm sure you'd love her.

BERTUCCIO.
Did you learn her name?

FIORDELISA.
I asked it, first, to set it in my prayers,
And then, that *you* might pray for her.

BERTUCCIO.
Her name? [*Aside.*] I pray! [*Contemptuously.*

FIORDELISA.
The Countess Malatesta.

BERTUCCIO (*aside*).
Count Malatesta's wife protect my child!
You have not seen her since?

FIORDELISA.
No; though she urged me
So hard to come to her; and asked my name,
And who my parents were, and where I lived.

BERTUCCIO.
You did not tell her?

FIORDELISA.
Who my parents were?
How could I, when I must not know myself?

BERTUCCIO.
Patience, my darling; trust thy father's love,
That there is reason for this mystery!

The time may come when we may live in peace,
And walk together free, under free heaven
But that cannot be here — nor now!

FIORDELISA.
                              Oh, when —
When shall that time arrive?

             BERTUCCIO (*bitterly*).
                              When what I live for
Has been achieved!

             FIORDELISA (*timidly*).
                    What *you* live for?

             BERTUCCIO (*with sudden ferocity*).
                                        Revenge!

    FIORDELISA (*averting her eyes with horror*).
Oh, do not look so, father!

                    BERTUCCIO.
                         Listen, girl,
You asked me of your mother; it is time
You should know why all questioning of her
Racks me to madness. Look upon me, child;
Misshapen as I am, there once was one,
Who, seeing me despised, mocked, lonely, poor,
Loved me, I think, most for my misery;
Thy mother, like thee, just so pure, so sweet.
I was a public notary in Cesena;
Our life was humble, but so happy; thou
Wert in thy cradle then, and many a night
Thy mother and I sat hand-in-hand together,
Watching thine innocent smiles, and building up
Long plans of joy to come!
                    [*His voice falters; he turns away.*

FIORDELISA.
Alas! she died.

BERTUCCIO.
Died! There are deaths 't is comfort to look back on;
Hers was not such a death. A devil came
Across our quiet life, and marked her beauty,
And lusted for her; and when she scorned his offers,
Because he was a noble, great and strong,
He bore her from my side, by force, and after
I never saw her more; they brought me news
That she was dead.

FIORDELISA.
Ah me!

BERTUCCIO.
And I was mad
For years and years, and when my wits came back —
If e'er they came — they brought one haunting purpose
That since has shaped my life, — to have revenge!
Revenge upon her wronger and his order;
Revenge in kind; to quit him, — wife for wife!

FIORDELISA.
Father, 't is not for me to question with you;
But think! revenge belongeth not to man
It is God's attribute, usurp it not!

BERTUCCIO.
Preach abstinence to him that dies of hunger,
Tell the poor wretch who perishes of thirst,
There 's danger in the cup his fingers clutch;
But bid me not forswear revenge. No word!
Thou know'st now why I mew thee up so close;
Keep thee out of the streets; shut thee from eyes

And tongues of lawless men, — for in these days
All men are lawless, —'t is because I fear
To lose thee, as I lost thy mother.

FIORDELISA.

       Father,
I 'll pray for her.

BERTUCCIO.

     Do, and for me; good-night!

FIORDELISA.

Oh, not so soon, with all these sad dark thoughts,
These bitter memories. You need my love;
I 'll touch my lute for you, and sing to it.
Music, you know, chases all evil angels.

BERTUCCIO.

I must go: 't is grave business calls me hence.
[*Aside.*] 'T is time that I was at my post. My own,
Sleep in thine innocence. Good! good-night!

FIORDELISA.

But let me see you to the outer door.

BERTUCCIO.

Not a step further, then. God guard this place,
That here my flower may grow, safe from the blight
Of look, or word impure, — a holy thing
Consecrate to my service, and my love!
[*Exit* BERTUCCIO *and* FIORDELISA, R. *Enter from behind
 the arras,* MANFREDI *and* TORELLI.

MANFREDI.

His daughter! That so fair a branch should spring
From such a gnarled and misshapen stock!

TORELLI.

But did you mark how he raved of revenge
Upon our order?

MANFREDI.

By the mass, I think
That Guido Malatesta is the man
That played him the shrewd trick he told the girl of
'T was at Cesena, marked you — the time fits.
That's why he hounds me on after the Countess
What! must I be the tool of his revenge?
I'll teach the scurrile slave to strike at nobles.

TORELLI.

Hark! what's that? [*Listening.*

MANFREDI.

'T is outside the window.

TORELLI (*listening*).

Yes,
By Bacchus, some one climbs the balcony.

MANFREDI.

A gallant?

TORELLI.

In, sir; see the play played out.

MANFREDI.

But I'll not be forestalled!

TORELLI.

We've time enough.
[*They retire to the recess. Enter* DELL' AQUILA *from the balcony.*

DELL' AQUILA.

Pardon, sweet saint, if I profane thy shrine.
I watched Bertuccio forth; he passed me close,
I feared he would have seen me. I have sworn
Not to betray their foul design to him,
And to warn her, this means alone is left me.
Hark! 't is her gracious step, she comes this way.
[*Enter* FIORDELISA; *she kneels before the statue of the Madonna.*

FIORDELISA.

Comfort of the afflicted, comfort *him!*
Turn his revengeful purpose to submission,
And grant that I may grow to take the place
My mother has left empty in his heart!
He's gone! And I had not the heart to speak
Of the young gentleman who follows me.
He asked if any spoke to me; I told
The truth, — he never spoke to me.
[*Turning round and seeing* DELL' AQUILA.
[*In great terror.*] Who's there?
Brigitta! help!

DELL' AQUILA.

Silence! but have no fear.
I am not here to harm you, do not tremble.
I would die, lady, rather than offend you.

FIORDELISA.

Oh, sir, how came you here?

DELL' AQUILA.

I knew no other way
But by the balcony. Desperate occasions
Dispense with ceremony. My respect
Is absolute. Fear not: I am not here

To say, "I love you," nor to tell you how
For months your face has been my beacon star.
My passion never would have found a tongue;
It is too reverent; but your safety, lady,
I can be bold for that.

FIORDELISA.
My safety!

DELL' AQUILA.
Threatened
With desperate danger. Think you one so fair
Could even pray in safety in Faenza?
You have been seen: your beauty hath been buzzed
In the Court's amorous ear. There is a project
To scale your balcony to-night.

FIORDELISA.
Oh, father!

DELL' AQUILA.
He cannot save you. What were his sole strength
Against the bravos that the duke commands,
For any deed of ill? My arm and sword
Are stronger than your father's, and are yours
As absolutely. And yet what were these?
I could die for you, but I could not save you.

FIORDELISA.
What shall I do?

DELL' AQUILA.
Have you no friends, protectors,
To whom you might betake yourself?

FIORDELISA.
Alas!
I am a stranger here.

DELL' AQUILA.
Think, have you none?

FIORDELISA.
Ha! if the Countess Malatesta —

DELL' AQUILA.
What?
You know her?

FIORDELISA.
She once rescued me from insult
Of a rude man, and promised help whene'er
I chose to seek it.

DELL' AQUILA.
She is good and pure
And powerful, moreover. That's the chief.
Go to her straight; you have no time to lose.
Midnight is fixed for their foul enterprise.

FIORDELISA.
But how to find the house? And then the streets
Are dark and dangerous. I've but our servant,
Brigitta —

DELL' AQUILA.
Not a word to her! She's false.
Can you trust me? I'll lead you to the Countess.

FIORDELISA (*aside*).
Were this a stratagem!

DELL' AQUILA.
I see you doubt me;
I know you have good cause to doubt all men.
Oh, could I bare my heart, and show you there

Your image set amongst its holiest thoughts,
Beside my mother's well-remembered face.
Could truth speak with the tongue, look from the eyes,
You would not doubt me! What can oaths avail?
He who could cheat you, would not fear to cheat
God and his saints! Lady, it is the truth
That I have spoken! May Heaven give you faith
To trust me.; but if not, I will stay,
And die in your defence.

FIORDELISA.

     Sir, I will trust you!
And Heaven so deal with you as you with me!
Go with me to the Countess Malatesta.
I'll seek the shelter of her roof to-night,
To-morrow must bring counsel for the future.

DELL' AQUILA.

Oh! bless you for this trust! Come, quick, but softly.
Put on your veil, fear not, I am your guard,
Your slave, your sentinel. I crave no guerdon,
Not even a look! Enough for me to save you.
    [*Exit* FIORDELISA *and* DELL' AQUILA

MANFREDI (*breaking from behind the arras;* TORELLI
   following him).

Why did you hold me back? Our project's marred.
This moonstruck poet bears away the prize,
And I am fooled.

TORELLI.

   Nay, trust my cooler brain.
I'll follow him to Malatesta's. Sure,
He'll give her shelter?

MANFREDI.
In his lady's absence?

TORELLI.
Even so. The old ruffian can be courteous
When there 's a pretty face in question!

MANFREDI.
Let him!
I 'll break his house, or any man that dares
Set his locks in the way of my good pleasure!

TORELLI.
Why not? 'T will give a double pungency
To our revenge upon Bertuccio.
We only looked to keep the foul-mouthed knave
Out of the way while we bore off his pearl;
But now we 'll use him for the robbery.
He shall see *us* scale Malatesta's windows;
But she whom we bear thence, muffled and gagged,
Shall be the hunch-backed scoffer's pretty daughter!

MANFREDI.
A rare revenge! and so this brain-sick poet
And my curst jester may console each other.
Watch them to Malatesta's! I 'll to our friends,
And find Bertuccio by San Stefano!
[*Exit by secret door*, L. 2 E.

SCENE II.

*A street near the Church of San Stefano; stage dark.
Enter* BERTUCCIO, L., *cloaked and masked.*

BERTUCCIO.

The hour has struck, — they will be here anon, —
Trust them to keep tryst for a villainous deed.
I had need to whet the memory of my wrong,
Or my girl's angel face and innocent tongue
Had shaken even *my* steadfastness of purpose!
And Malatesta's wife has done her kindness, —
I would that she had not! But what's such slight service
To my huge wrong? Let me but think of that!
I grow too human near my child. I lack
The sharp sting of court scorn to spur the sides
Of my intent! With her I 'm free to weep,
With them, I still must laugh, — still be their ape,
To mop and mow and wake their shallow mirth.
True, I can sometimes bite, as monkeys do.
They 'll make mirth of that, too! O courtly sirs!
Sweet-spoken, stalwart gallants! if you knew
The hate that rankles underneath my motley,
The scorn that barbs my wit, the bitterness
That grins behind my laughter, you would start
And shudder o'er your cups, and cross yourselves
As if the devil were in your company!
Once my revenge achieved, I 'll spurn my chain,
Fool it no more, but give what 's left of life
To thought of her I 've lost, and love of her
That yet is left me.

[*Enter* MANFREDI, ASCOLTI, *and* ORDELAFFI, *masked and cloaked.*

MANFREDI.
Hist, Bertuccio!

BERTUCCIO.
Here, gossip Galeotto, — you are punctual;
Ascolti too; grave Signor Florentine,
We'll show you how the gallants of Faenza
Treat greybeards who aspire to handsome wives.
Remember your beard's grizzled — and beware —

ASCOLTI.
I will stand warned. You have the ladders here?

BERTUCCIO.
The lackeys wait in charge of them hard by.
But where's Torelli? we shall want his help.

ORDELAFFI.
Pshaw! our three swords are plenty.

BERTUCCIO.
Cry you mercy!
'T is not Torelli's sword we want.

ORDELAFFI.
What then?

BERTUCCIO.
His marvellous quick scent of danger, man.
Stick to *his* skirts, I'll answer for 't you're safe.
Perhaps he smelt some risk of buffets here,
And so has ta'en him home to bed.

MANFREDI.
Away
Towards Malatesta's house! 't was there he promised

To meet us. Sirrah fool, be it thy post
To hold the ladder while we mount; and see
Thou play'st us no jade's trick, or 'ware the whip.

BERTUCCIO.

Fear not, magnanimous gossip! do your work
With as good will as I do mine. The Countess
Sleeps in the chamber of the balcony
Which rounds the angle of the southern front;
I came but now by the palace, — all was quiet.

MANFREDI.

Set on, then, cautiously, — use not your swords,
Unless on strong compulsion; blood tells tales,
And I want no more feuds upon my hands. [*Exeunt,* R.

SCENE III.

Exterior of the palace of MALATESTA, *with street. The flat exhibits the corner of two streets. The palace of* MALATESTA *is on a set piece,* L. U. E. *A window on the first floor, with a balcony, practicable.* — *Night. Enter* FIORDELISA *and* DELL' AQUILA, *followed by* TORELLI *at a distance. Through the scene between* FIORDELISA, DELL' AQUILA, *and* MALATESTA, TORELLI *watches and listens behind a projecting piece of masonry.*

DELL' AQUILA.

Be of good cheer, — this is the house; I'll knock,
And summon forth the Count.   [*Knocks.*

FIORDELISA.

     Oh, sir! what thanks
Can e'er repay this kindness?

DELL' AQUILA.

       But remember
Who 't was that did it, I am thanked enough.

FIORDELISA.

I 'll pray for you after my father — hark!

DELL' AQUILA.

They come!   [*Enter a Servant from house.*
    Two strangers who crave instant speech
Of the Count Malatesta.   [*Exit Servant.*

DELL' AQUILA.

And I should see your father?

FIORDELISA.

       Then you know him?

DELL' AQUILA.

Yes.

FIORDELISA.

  And his business — occupations?   [*He bows.*
[*Sadly.*] 'T is more than I do, sir, that am his child.
I do not even know his name.

DELL' AQUILA.

      What he
Keeps secret from you 't is not mine to tell;
'T were well you should not question him too closely;
He shall learn you are safe.

FIORDELISA.

      And tell him, too,
That 't was *you* saved me, sir. Promise me that!
      [*Enter* MALATESTA, L

MALATESTA.

Who is it would have speech of Malatesta?

DELL' AQUILA.

You know me, Count?

MALATESTA.

Dell' Aquila, well met!
But your companion? [*Aside.*] Ha! a petticoat!
So ho, my poet!

DELL' AQUILA.

Pardon, if I pray
This lady's name may rest a secret, Count;
She is in grievous danger, — one from which
Your house can shelter her. She owes already
Your countess much, for good help given at need,
So craves to increase the debt.

MALATESTA.

My house is hers.
But she should know my countess is not here.

FIORDELISA.

Not here!

MALATESTA.

But if she dare trust my grey hairs
She shall have shelter.

DELL' AQUILA.

Nay, she cannot choose.

MALATESTA.

I'll give her my wife's chamber, if she will;
Her woman to attend her.

DELL' AQUILA.
All she needs
Is your roof's shelter for the night; to-morrow
Must see her otherwise bestowed.

MALATESTA.
Go in,
Fair lady; my poor house, with all that's in it,
Is at your service. Had my wife been here,
You had had gentler 'tendance; as it is,
I'll lead you to her chamber and there leave you.

TORELLI (*aside*).
Now to the hunters; I've marked down the deer.
[*Exit* TORELLI, L. U. E.

MALATESTA (*to* AQUILA).
You will not stay and crush a cup with me?

DELL' AQUILA.
No, not to-night.
[*To* FIORDELISA.] Did you not well to trust me?
Farewell; think of me in your prayers!

FIORDELISA.
I cannot
Choose but do that, sir. [*Aside.*] Oh, the thought of him
Will come, henceforth, betwixt my prayers and Heaven!
[*Exit* MALATESTA, L., *leading in* FIORDELISA.

DELL' AQUILA.
His child! Since when did grapes grow upon thistles?
And yet I'm glad to know the tie that binds
The two together such a holy one!
Sweet angel, — sister angels guard thy sleep!

Now to seek out Bertuccio, and tell him
The danger she has 'scaped, and thank the saints
That made *me* her preserver.

[*Exit* DELL' AQUILA, R. *Enter cautiously,* L. U. E., BER
TUCCIO, MANFREDI, ASCOLTI, ORDELAFFI, *and* TORELLI
with Servants carrying ladders.

MANFREDI.

Softly, you knaves! with velvet tread, like tigers —

BERTUCCIO.

Say rather, "cats."

[*A light appears at the window,* L. 2 E.

TORELLI.

Which is the balcony?

BERTUCCIO (*pointing*).

That! I have noted in this summer weather
The window's left unbarred.

ASCOLTI.

Ha! there's a light!
If she were stirring!

BERTUCCIO.

What an' if she were?
A sudden spring, — a cloak flung o'er her head;
If she have time to scream, you are but bunglers.

MANFREDI.

My cloak will serve. [*Takes it off*

ASCOLTI.

If she alarm the house
It might go hard with us.

BERTUCCIO.

                          O cats that long
For fish, yet fear to wet your feet! I 'll shame you.
Let me mount first; give me your cloak, Galeotto!

MANFREDI.

By your leave, fool, I 'll net my own bird. Back!
Hold thou the ladder; that is lackeys' work,
And fits thee best. Ascolti and Torelli,
Guard the approaches! I and Ordelaffi
Will be enough to mount, and snare the game.
[*The light is extinguished; the Servants set a ladder to
  the balcony.*

BERTUCCIO (*holds it*).

All 's dark now, — up!

MANFREDI.

                    Why, rogue, how thy hand shakes!
Is 't fear?

BERTUCCIO.

'T is inward laughter, Galeotto.
To think how blank Guido will look to-morrow
To find the nest cold, and his mate borne off.
[MANFREDI *mounts the ladder, followed by* ORDELAFFI.
  They enter the balcony.

BERTUCCIO (*eagerly listening*).

Ha! they are in by this time!
                            Cautious fools!
I had done 't myself in half the space! So, Guido,
You love your young wife well, they say; that 's brave.

[MANFREDI *and* ORDELAFFI *appear on the balcony, bearing*
  FIORDELISA *in their arms, muffled in* MANFREDI'S
  cloak. She struggles, but cannot scream. ORDELAFFI
  descends first, MANFREDI *hands* FIORDELISA *to him.*
  They come down the ladder.

BERTUCCIO.

'T is done!

MANFREDI.

   Away all, — to my garden house,
There to bestow our prize!
[*Exeunt* MANFREDI *and* ORDELAFFI, L. U. E. — *The Servants carry off the ladder.*

BERTUCCIO.

    Now, Malatesta,
   [*Shaking his fist at the house.*
Learn what it is to wake and find her gone
That was the pride and joy of your dim eyes, —
The comfort of your age! I welcome you
To the blank hearth, — the hunger of the soul, —
The long dark days and miserable nights!
These you gave me; I give them back to you!
I, the despised, deformed, dishonoured jester,
Have reached up to your crown and pulled it down,
And flung it in the mire, as you flung mine!
Now, murdered innocent, *thou* art avenged!
But I have private wrongs, too, to repay;
This proud Manfredi, — he you spat upon,
He you spurned such a day, set in the stocks,
Whipped, — *he* is even with your mightiness!
Here is Francesca's ring; and here the letter,
To tell her that *her* vengeance, too, is ripe.
The blow shall come from her, but mine's the hand
That guides the dagger's point straight to *his* heart!
I cannot sleep! I'll walk the night away;
It is no night for me, — my day has come! [*Exit*, R.

ACT III.

SCENE. — *A room in the garden-house of* GALEOTTO MANFREDI, *decorated with arabesques in the style of the earlier renaissance, — folding-doors at the back, communicating with an inner chamber; side entrances,* R. *and* L., *covered by curtains; a table, and chairs of the curule form.*

SCENE I.

Enter FIORDELISA, *from* R.

FIORDELISA (*pressing her hands to her temples*).
Where am I? What has happened? let me think!
Those men! — that blinding veil, — the fresh night air
That struck upon my face! Then a wild struggle,
In strong and mastering arms! Then a long blank!
I must have fainted; when I woke I lay
On a rich couch in that room. Has he brought me
Into the very danger that he said
He came to take me from? Oh, cruel! No;
Falsehood could ne'er have found such words, such looks.
Father! — oh, when he comes and finds me gone!
I must go hence!
 [*Looking round.*] That door! —
  [*She runs to side entrance,* L.] 'T is locked!
      [*Shaking door.*] Help! help!
How dare they draw their bolts on me! My father
Shall punish them for this! I will go forth!
  [*Shakes door again; the door opens from without.*
At last! — Whoe'er you are, sir, help me hence!
      [*Enter* MANFREDI, L.

Take me back to my father! He will bless you !
Reward you —

MANFREDI.
   Nay, your own lips must do that.

FIORDELISA.
Oh, they shall bless you too, sir —

MANFREDI.
        To be blessed
With that sweet mouth were well, yet scarce enough.

FIORDELISA.
Oh, sir, we waste time! Set what price you will
On the great service, I am sure my father
Will pay you.   [MANFREDI *re-locks the door*

MANFREDI.
     If we're to discuss your ransom
'T were fairest we should do it with closed doors;
The terms can scarce be settled till you know
Your prison, jailer, in what risk you stand.
First, for your prison, — Know you where you are?

FIORDELISA.
No.

MANFREDI.
  In the Duke Manfredi's palace. Next,
Know you your jailer?

FIORDELISA.
   Who?

MANFREDI.
        Manfredi's self.

FIORDELISA (*wringing her hands*).

Woe's me!

MANFREDI.

What? Is the news so terrible?

FIORDELISA.

I've heard Brigitta, and my father, too,
Speak of the Duke Manfredi.

MANFREDI (*aside*).

Here's a chance
To hear a genuine judgment of myself!
[*To her.*] They said —

FIORDELISA.

That he was cruel, bold, unsated
In thirst for evil pleasures, — it was odds
Whether more feared or hated in Faenza.

MANFREDI (*aside*).

Trust the crowd's garlic cheers and greasy caps!
The knaves shall know me worse ere they have done.
I thank you, pretty one, — I am the Duke!

FIORDELISA.

Then Heaven have mercy on me!

MANFREDI.

If report
Speak truth, your prayer were idle! — but report
Is a sad liar. Do I look the ogre
They painted to you? Nay, my fluttered dove,
Smooth but those ruffled feathers; look about you!
Is this so grim a dungeon? Was your couch

Last night so hard, — your 'tendance so ungentle?
I am *your* prisoner, fairest, — not you mine.

FIORDELISA.

Then let me go!

MANFREDI.

Not till you know at least
What you will lose by going. All Faenza
Is mine, and she I favour may command
Whate'er Faenza holds of wealth or pleasure.
I'll pour them at her feet, and after fling
Myself there too, to woo a gracious word!
What's life, ungraced by love? — a dismal sky
Without sun, moon, or starlight! 'T is a cup
Drained of the wine that reddened in its gold!
A lute shorn of its strings, — a table stripped
Of all its festal meats, — mere life in death
A jewel like thy beauty is not meet
To be shut in a chest; it should be set
To shine in princely robes, — to grace a crown.
I would set thee in mine. [*Approaching her.*

FIORDELISA.

Stand back, my lord!

MANFREDI.

Why, little fool, I would not harm a hair
On thy fair head. Think what thy life has been!
How dull and dark and dreary! It shall be
As bright and glad and sunny as the prime
Of summer flowers. Only repel not joy
Because it comes borne in the hand of Love!

FIORDELISA.

Oh, you profane that name! Is Love the friend
Of night and violence and robbery?

Let me go hence, I say! I have a father
Who'll make you terribly aby this wrong,
Lord as you are!

MANFREDI.

           Your father! By the Mass!
She makes me laugh! Your father, girl! Bertuccio!

FIORDELISA.

That I should learn my father's name from him!
Yes, Duke, my father!

MANFREDI.

              Why, he is my slave, —
A thing that crouches to me like my hound,
To beg for food, or deprecate the lash, —
My butt, — my whipping-block, — my fool in motley!

FIORDELISA.

It is *not* true! This is a lie, like all
That you have said. Let me go forth, I say!

MANFREDI.

You're in my palace. Here are none but those
To whom my will is law; your calls for help
Will only bring more force, — if I could stoop
To use force with a lady —

FIORDELISA.

              Then you *have*
Some manhood in you. Look, sir, at us two.
You are a duke, you say, — your power but bounded
By your own will. I am a poor weak girl,
E'en weaker than I knew, if what you say
Touching my father be the truth. What honour
Is to be won on me? Yet, won it may be,

By yielding to my prayers to be set free, —
To be sent home.   Oh, let me but go hence
As I came hither; I will speak to none
Of this night's outrage, — even to my father.

MANFREDI.

Ask anything but this.

FIORDELISA.

Nothing but this!
You have a wife, my lord; what if she knew?

MANFREDI.

The more need to take care that you tell her not!
Come, little one, give up these swelling looks,
Though they become you mightily.

[*Approaching her.*

FIORDELISA.

Stand off!
[*He pursues her; she flies*
Help!   Help!   [*Running to the* C. *door.*
A door! ha!
[*She forces it open, rushes in, and closes it violently.*

MANFREDI (*locking it outside*).

Deeper in the toils!
[*Laughs.*]   The lamb seeks shelter in the wolf's own den.

TORELLI (*at* L. *door outside*).

My lord!

MANFREDI (*unlocks the door*)
Torelli's voice!   How now, Torelli?
[*Enter* TORELLI, L.

TORELLI.

My lord, the Duchess is returned.

MANFREDI.

                        Why, man,
Thy news is stale; the Duchess has been here
These five hours; she arrived, post-haste, ere sunrise.
She must have ridden in the dark. 'T was that
Prevented me from making earlier matins
Before my little saint here.

TORELLI.

                    Do you know
What brought the Duchess back so suddenly?

MANFREDI.

Some jealous fancy pricked her, as I judge
From her accost when we encountered first;
And, as I gathered, she suspects contrivance
Betwixt me and the Countess Malatesta.
'T was a relief, for once, that I could twit her
With groundless fears. I told her Malatesta
Rode yesterday with his lady to Cesena,
And, for more proof, repeated what he said,
That on my wife's least summons, she'd return;
So she *has* summoned her, in hopes, no doubt,
To catch me in a lie. Her messenger
Rode to Cesena just at daybreak. Soon
We may look for him back, bringing, I hope,
Ginevra Malatesta.

TORELLI.

                This is rare.
So falls she off the scent, and leaves you here
To follow up your game with Fiordelisa.

MANFREDI.

Even so; I excused me from her presence
By work of State, for which to this pavilion

I had summoned you and the envoy of Florence, —
Staid work of State, being no less a one
Than to lend me your presences at the banquet
I mean to offer our fair prisoner.
Bid Ordelaffi and Ascolti hither,
And send my men with fruits and wines and sweetmeats,—
All that is likeliest to tempt the sense
Of this scared bird.

TORELLI.

How did you find her, sir?

MANFREDI.

Beating her pretty wings against the bars;
Still calling for her father. Shrewdly minded
To peck, instead of kissing, silly fledgeling!
But I will tame her yet, till she shall come
To perch upon my finger.

TORELLI.

Where is she?

MANFREDI.

In the inner room, whither she fled but now.
Fear not, — I turned the key on her; she's safe.

TORELLI.

I'll send what you command, and warn the rest
That you attend them. Good speed to your wooing!
[*Exit* TORELLI, *by entrance*, L.

MANFREDI.

Now for my prisoner! by gentle means
To gain her ear. Asmodeus, tip my tongue
With love's persuasion.

[*Exit into inner room,* C. *Enter* THE DUCHESS FRANCESCA, *masked, and* BERTUCCIO, *who has resumed his fool's dress,* R.

FRANCESCA (*unmasking*).

Was 't not Torelli went hence, even now?

BERTUCCIO.

By the great walk? I think it was. Be sure
He saw us not in the pleached laurel alley.

FRANCESCA.

Then you still bear me out, my husband lies?
That Malatesta's wife has *not* gone hence?

BERTUCCIO.

Trust a fool's eyes before a husband's tongue.
I say again, I was at hand last night
When your lord bore from Malatesta's house
Saïd Malatesta's wife. I saw the deed.
I heard the order given to bring her hither.

FRANCESCA.

Then 't was by force, not by the lady's will,
She came?

BERTUCCIO.

      Force? Quotha, — force? How many ladies
Have had to bless the " force " that saved their tongue
An awkward " yes! " See you not what an answer
" Force " finds for all? It stops a husband's mouth;
Crams its fist down the town's throat; nay, at a pinch,
Perks its sufficient self in a wife's face.
Commend me still to " force." It saves more credits
Than e'er it ruined virtues. After folly,
I hold force the best mask that wit has found
To mock the world with!

FRANCESCA.
                              There's weight in that.
This violence would stand her in good stead,
Were she e'er called in question! Then what matter,
[BERTUCCIO, *who has been moving round the room, stops opposite centre door.*
So I be wronged, if 't is by force or will!
Would I had certain proof!

BERTUCCIO.
                              Ha! you want proof?
Come here!   [THE DUCHESS *approaches him.*
       Stand where I stand. Now listen, — close.

FRANCESCA (*listening at door*).
My husband's voice in passionate entreaty!

BERTUCCIO.
Only *his* voice?
       FRANCESCA (*starting*).
              An answering voice! a woman's!
These are your State affairs, my gracious duke!

BERTUCCIO.
If you would have more proof, I'll bring you where
You shall hear his humble tools in last night's business
Discuss the deed, — all noble gentlemen,
Who'd pluck my hood about my ears if I
Durst hint a doubt of their veracity.

FRANCESCA.
Do so; and if they bear thy story out,
I know my part.
       BERTUCCIO.
              What! tears?

FRANCESCA.
            Tears? Death to both!

BERTUCCIO.
Take care! His guards are faithful. Can you trust
A hand to do the deed?

FRANCESCA.
        I trust my own.

BERTUCCIO.
Women turn pale at blood. Your heart may fail you
When the time comes to strike.

FRANCESCA.
            Daggers for men!
I know a surer weapon.

   BERTUCCIO (*creeping up to her and whispering*).
        Poison?

    FRANCESCA (*putting her finger on her lip*).
            Hush!
The Borgia's physician gave it me!
It may be trusted!

            BERTUCCIO (*withdrawing, aside*).
            My she leopard's loosed!
                    [*Exit* BERTUCCIO, L.

    FRANCESCA (*still at the door*, C., *listening*).
Past doubt, a woman's tongue! And now my husband's
How well I know the soft, smooth, pleading voice, —
The voice that drew my young heart to my lips
When, at my father's court, I plighted troth

To him, and he to me! Oh, bitterness!
Now spurned for each new leman of the hour!
Oh, he shall learn how terrible is hate
That grows of love abused!
[*Taking a phial from her bosom.*
Come, bosom friend,
That hast lain cold, of late, against my heart,
As if to whisper to it, "Be thou stone,
When the time calls for *me*." [*Looking at the phial.*
Each drop's a death!
What matter who she be? Enough for me
That she usurps the place that should be mine
In Galeotto's love! Hark! some one comes.
[*She conceals the phial, and resumes her mask. Enter two Chamberlains with white wands, L., followed by Attendants bearing a banquet, and pass into the inner room; after them a* PAGE, *with wine in a golden flagon; goblets, fruit, etc., on a salver. She stops him as he is going through the folding-doors.*
Hold, sir; set down your charge.

PAGE.

By your leave, madame:
'T is for my lord.

FRANCESCA.

Since when was that an answer
To give thy lady? [*Removes her mask.*
PAGE (*aside*).
'T is the Duchess! [*Respectfully.*] Pardon,
I knew you not.

FRANCESCA.

Enough, sir, set it down,
And wait without till I bid thee bear in.
[*Exit* PAGE, L., *after placing the salver on the table.*
What need of further proof? Is 't heaven or hell

That sends this apt occasion? Galeotto,
I warned thee in the springtime of our loves,
This hand could kill as easy as caress;
You laughed, and took it in your ampler palm,
And said that death were pleasant from such white
And taper fingers. Try it now!
[*She pours some of the contents of the phial into the flagons
of wine.*

        'T is done!
      [*Re-enter* BERTUCCIO, L., *hastily.*

BERTUCCIO.

Hide, here, Madonna: here their lordships come!
I met them on the way, so brave and merry!
My gossip Galeotto bids them here,
To feast with him and *her!*
[*Exit* BERTUCCIO L. FRANCESCA *starts as if stung, then
goes to the door and beckons. Re-enter,* PAGE, L.
She signs to him: he bears in the wine.

FRANCESCA (*aside*).
       Their doom is sealed!
[*She retires behind curtained entrance,* R. *Re-enter* BER-
TUCCIO, *with* ASCOLTI *and* ORDELAFFI, L.

BERTUCCIO.

It is your due; you that go out bat-fowling
Lack wine o' mornings to keep up your hearts.

ORDELAFFI.

Why, thou wert there, knave; yet try thou to enter
Into the presence, and they 'll whip thee back;
His Highness wants no fool to-day!

BERTUCCIO.

That's true, —
With you two for his company. But tell me,
How will the lady relish, o'er her wine,
The cut-throat faces that she saw last night?
Methinks 't will mar her appetite.

ASCOLTI.

Be sure
She will not look so scared at *us*
As *thou* would'st at the sight of *her*.

BERTUCCIO.

Who — I?
Nay, I but held the ladder; we poor knaves
Must take the leavings of your rogueries,
As of your feasts; but prithee, Ordelaffi,
How looked she in her night-rail?

ORDELAFFI.

Would'st believe it?
Methought she had a something of thy favour,
As — if so crook'd a thing could have a daughter —
Thy daughter might have had.

[*All laugh.* BERTUCCIO *starts.*

ASCOLTI.

How now? He winces!
There cannot, sure, be issue of thy loins!
Nature's too merciful; she broke the mould
When she turned *thee* out!

BERTUCCIO.

Nature, sir, proportions
Her witty fools to her dull ones; while she makes
Ascoltis, she must needs produce Bertuccios

To sting their hard hides now and then. But tell me,
Think you Ginevra needed all that force?

ORDELAFFI.

She struggled stoutly; but a lady's struggles,
I take it, are much like her "no," — which often
Must be read "yes."

ASCOLTI.

Let's in, at once, my lords.

BERTUCCIO.

I'll marshal you. Who said that cap and bells
Should be shut out?

ASCOLTI.

Stand back, Sir Fool; 't were best.
You may repent your pressing on too far.

BERTUCCIO.

I fain would see the lady; 't is not often
That one can carry a beauty off at night,
And make her laugh i' the morning.

ORDELAFFI.

Neither she
Nor you, I think, are likely to breed much mirth
Out of each other.

BERTUCCIO.

Say you so? Here goes!
[*He runs up to the door; a* PAGE *opens it and motions him back, two Chamberlains appearing at the open door.*
Why, how now, sirrah? I'm the fool!

PAGE.

Stand back!

BERTUCCIO.

I! — why I'm free o' the palace; every place
Except the council chamber, and in that
I sit by proxy!

PAGE.

'T is the Duke's strict order
You enter not this room.
[BERTUCCIO *is pressing forward.*
Back! or the grooms
Shall score thy hunch to motley. [*He closes the door.*

ASCOLTI.

How now, sirrah!
Call you this marshalling?

BERTUCCIO.

I am right served!
I forgot that fools in silks should take precedence
Of fools in motley! Lead the way, my lords!

ORDELAFFI.

Look! here comes Malatesta.

BERTUCCIO.

Ha! — but stay,
To hear me gird at him! You call me bitter;
Now you shall see how merciful I've been.

ASCOLTI.

Waste not your ears on him; the Duke awaits us
Beside his beauty, — metal more attractive
Than this cursed word-catcher.

ORDELAFFI.

Ay, ay! let's in
[*Exeunt* ORDELAFFI *and* ASCOLTI. BERTUCCIO *goes hastily to* R. *entrance. Enter* FRANCESCA.

BERTUCCIO.

Now, now, Madonna, have you proof enough?

FRANCESCA.

Mountains of proof on proof, if proof were needed;
But had disproof come with them, and not proof,
'T is all too late.

BERTUCCIO.

  How?

FRANCESCA.

      I have drugged their wine
They will sleep sound to-night. [*She retires up stage.*

BERTUCCIO (*aside*).

       Choose woman's hands,
You that would have grim work nimbly dispatched!
Here 's Malatesta, — looking black as night!
So, Lord, I hope you liked your waking news?
Now — now — to gloat over his agony!

      [*Enter* MALATESTA, L.

MALATESTA (*not seeing* THE DUCHESS).

Ha, knave, I 'd see the Duchess.

  BERTUCCIO (*looking at him curiously*).
      Marvellous!

MALATESTA.

How now?

BERTUCCIO.

   To think that they can make such caps
To hide all trace of them!

MALATESTA.

    Of what knave?

BERTUCCIO.
                                        Horns.

MALATESTA.

Rascal!

BERTUCCIO.
        I hope your lordship had good rest,
And that my lady, too, slept undisturbed?

MALATESTA.

What mean you, sirrah?

BERTUCCIO.
                Nay, strain not so hard
To keep it down; you are among friends here.
A grievous loss, no doubt; but at your age
You could scarce look to keep her to yourself.
Others have lost wives, too, — poor knaves who thought
To stick in their thrum-caps jewels that caught
The eyes of nobles; needs were they must yield
Daughters or wives —

MALATESTA.
                Art mad, or drunk, or both?
My errand's to thy mistress, not to thee.
Where is she?

FRANCESCA (*coming down stage*).
        Here, my lord!   [*They talk apart.*

BERTUCCIO.
                He bears it bravely,
But wounds will bleed under an iron corselet:
And how his must be bleeding! For he loved her —
The whole Court vouches it — as old men love,
Husbanding their spent fires into a heat,
The fiercer that it has short time to burn.
        [FRANCESCA *and* MALATESTA *come forward.*

FRANCESCA.

You say your lady slept not here, last night,
But at Cesena?

MALATESTA.

Or the devil's in 't.
I saw her safe bestowed there; I can trust
My own eyes, — or still better, my own bolts.

BERTUCCIO (*amazed and aside*).

Is this old man, too, of Manfredi's council,
To cheat his wife?

MALATESTA.

I little thought to bring her back so soon,
But on your summons, I have straight recalled her.

BERTUCCIO (*breaking in eagerly*).

And she is here; hold him to that, Madonna!

MALATESTA.

Malapert dog!

FRANCESCA.

Pardon his licensed tongue.
I fain would see the lady.

MALATESTA (*bowing*).

You shall see her;
I have not far to fetch her. [*Exit* L

BERTUCCIO (*furiously*).

'T is a lie, —
A cursed lie, to hide his own foul shame!
Believe him not!

FRANCESCA.

But if he bring the lady?

BERTUCCIO (*laughing*).

Ay, if he bring the lady, then believe him!
[*Aside.*]   He robs me of my right, — taking his wrong
With outward show of calm: *mine* turned my brain.
I looked to see him mad, or drive him so!

MANFREDI (*within*).

More wine, knave!
[*Enter a* PAGE *from* C. *door, passes out* L.

FRANCESCA.

Ginevra, or another, — what of that?
The wrong's the same; why not the same revenge?

BERTUCCIO.

The same to you, but not the same to me!
I tell you, Malatesta's wife sits yonder, —
Sits at your husband's side; I saw her — I —
Borne off last night!   I *saw!*   There is no faith
In eyes or ears or truth, if 't were not she!
[*Re-enter* MALATESTA, L., *with* GINEVRA. BERTUCCIO'S *back is towards the door.*

MALATESTA.

Madame, my wife!

BERTUCCIO (*turning in amaze*).

Ginevra here! Then who
Was that they carried from her bed last night?
Who is 't sits yonder?

FRANCESCA.

Tell me, gracious lady,
Where did you sleep last night?

GENEVRA.

Where I scarce thought
To leave so soon, your Highness; in Cesena,
Within my husband's castle.

FRANCESCA.

Pardon, madame,
That I have set you on a hurried journey,
Still more that *I* have wronged you in my thoughts!
[*Passing her hand over her brow. Laughter heard within.*
[*Aside.*] They laugh! Laugh on, my lord, while it is
time.

GINEVRA.

Will 't please you, grant me audience; you shall hear
To the minute how my hours went yesterday,
Down to this moment.

FRANCESCA.

Come out in the air;
I stifle within hearing of their mirth.
[*To* BERTUCCIO.] Stay here; see that the other 'scape
me not. [*Exit* FRANCESCA *and* GINEVRA, L.

BERTUCCIO.

The other! Not Ginevra?
[*To* MALATESTA.] Good, my lord,
Your wife slept at Cesena, yet her chamber
Was not untenanted last night, I'll swear!

MALATESTA.

And so thou might'st, yet break no oath.

BERTUCCIO.

Who slept in 't?

MALATESTA.

I know not. Ask Dell' Aquila; 't was he
Brought me the lady, craving shelter for her
From some great danger.

BERTUCCIO.
    But you saw her face?

MALATESTA.

And if I did, think'st thou I 'd trust her name
To *thy* ass-ears?   [*Exit* MALATESTA, L.

BERTUCCIO.
   Fooled — mocked of my revenge!
The sweetest morsel on 't whipped from my teeth!
Oh, I could brain myself with my own bawble!
       [*Enter* DELL' AQUILA, L.
[*Aside.*] Dell' Aquila. *He* knows.

DELL' AQUILA.
      Well met, Bertuccio;
I 've sought thee since this morning, — nay, since midnight.

BERTUCCIO.

Ha!

DELL' AQUILA.

For a matter much concerns thy peace.
Thou hast a daughter. [BERTUCCIO *starts.*] How I know
 thou hast
Matters not to my story.

BERTUCCIO (*hastily*).
     Hush! hush! hush!
If you know this, as you 're a Christian man,
And poet, — poets should have softer hearts
Than courts and camps breed now-a-days, — oh, keep
The knowledge to yourself!

DELL' AQUILA.

      It is too late.
Torelli knew it; had set wolfish eyes
On her —

BERTUCCIO.
 Well? well?

DELL' AQUILA.

      Had rung her beauty's praise
Here in the Court. Thou hast no friends here.

BERTUCCIO (*eagerly*).

          Well?

DELL' AQUILA.
They plotted how to lure thee from the house,
And in thy absence to surprise her window,
And bear her off! They bound me by an oath
To keep it secret from *thee* — not from *her*.
I swore to save her or to lose myself,
So found a desperate means of speech with her,
And warned her of her danger.

BERTUCCIO.

      Thanks! thanks! thanks!
But only warned her!

DELL' AQUILA.
 Placed her, too, in safety.

BERTUCCIO.

Oh, heaven! where?

DELL' AQUILA.
  In the house of Malatesta.

BERTUCCIO (*hoarsely*).

My child in Malatesta's house last night?

DELL' AQUILA.

Secure;—even in the Countess's own chamber!

BERTUCCIO (*with a wild cry*).

My child! my child! wronged! murdered!

DELL' AQUILA.

Ha! by whom?

BERTUCCIO (*wildly*).

By me! by me! Her father—her own father!
That would have grasped Heaven's vengeance, and have drawn
The bolt on my own head, and hers—and hers!

DELL' AQUILA.

What do you mean?

BERTUCCIO.

I counselled the undoing
Of Malatesta's wife. I stood and watched,
And laughed for joy, and held the ladder for them;
And all the while 't was my own innocent child!
Look not so scared—'t is true; I am not mad!
She's here—now—in their clutches! [*Laughter within.*
Hark! they laugh.
'T is the hyænas o'er their prey—my child!—
And I stand here and cannot lift a hand!

DELL' AQUILA.

Here's mine, and my sword, too!

BERTUCCIO.

Oh, what were that
Against their felon blades?

DELL' AQUILA.

                True, true! what aid?
Ha, there's the Duchess!

BERTUCCIO (*shrieks*).

                I had forgotten her!
[*Drawing* DELL' AQUILA *to him and whispering hoarsely.*
Man, she has drugged their wine; the bony Death
Plays cupbearer to them: if she drinks, she dies!
                  [*Enter a* PAGE *with wine,* L.
Look! look! Perchance that is the very wine!
[*He runs between the* PAGE *and the door, and assumes the*
    FOOL'S *manner.*
Halt there! for the fool's toll. No wine goes in
But pays the fool's toll.

PAGE.

              Out knave! Stand aside!
[BERTUCCIO *snatches the flagons from the salver.*

BERTUCCIO.

'T is forfeit by the law!
[*The* PAGE *tries to recover the wine; in the struggle* BER-
    TUCCIO *pretends to upset the flagons by accident, and
    the wine is poured out on the stage.*

PAGE.

              Thy back shall bleed
To make it up. Now must I go fetch more, —
And brook the cellarer's chiding for thy folly.
                      [*Enter* TORELLI, L.

BERTUCCIO (*to* DELL' AQUILA).

If he goes in — could we but enter with him!
A word of mine might save her from the poison.
                [BERTUCCIO *gets between him and the door.*

TORELLI.

Good-day, Sir Poet; stand aside, Sir Fool.

BERTUCCIO.

You are going in?

TORELLI.

Ay!

BERTUCCIO.

There's a shrewd hiatus
Needs filling at the table. You have War
And Love, but, lacking Poetry and Folly,
War is but butchery, and Love goes lame.
Tuck us beneath your wings, sweet Baldassare,
And you'll be trebly welcome.
[*Seizing him by one arm, and motioning* DELL' AQUILA
  to take the other.

TORELLI.

The Duke for once has shut his doors against
Both Poetry and Folly. He is cloistered
For grave affairs.

BERTUCCIO.

Tush! tell me not, sweet gossip.
Why, man, *I* know that there's a petticoat —
And more, I know the wearer.

TORELLI.

Thou!

BERTUCCIO.

You've lost
The rarest sport. Ascolti and Ordelaffi
Have had their will of me. For once I'll own
You've turned the tables fairly on the fool!
That our Ginevra should be Fiordelisa.

And poor Bertuccio not know! Ha, ha!
Oh, excellent! It was a sleight of hand
I shall remember to my dying day.

TORELLI.

Nay, an' thou tak'st it so —

BERTUCCIO.

How should I take it?
Besides the pleasantness of it, there's the honour.
Think! my poor daughter in the Duke's high favour!
Why, there are counts by scores had pawned their
 'scutcheons
To come into such grace. I warrant now,
You thought I'd swear, and storm, and rend you all,
So shut me out. But, lo you! I am merry;
And so shall *she* be, if you'll let me in.
But let me in — I'll school the silly wench —
Teach her what honour she has come to; thank
The gracious duke, and play the merriest antics.
You'll swear you never saw me in such fooling —
But take me in.

TORELLI.

Why, now! the fool's grown wise!
I'll tell the Duke; perchance he'll let thee in.
[*Exit* TORELLI, C. BERTUCCIO, *exhausted by his emotions,
falls into a chair and writhes convulsively.*

DELL' AQUILA.

Lives hang on minutes here. Said you the Duchess
Had mixed the poison, or but meant to mix it?

BERTUCCIO.

There it is, man, — I know not which. E'en now
Death may be busy at her lips. Once in,

In my mad antics I might spurn the board,
And spill the flagons as I did e'en now;
But here I 'm helpless. Oh, Beelzebub!
Inspire them with desire to see a father
Make laughter of the undoing of his child!
Ha, some one comes! They 'll let me in!

[C. *door opens.*

TORELLI (*at the door*).

The Duke
Will none of thy ape's tricks.
[*He retires, closing the door.* BERTUCCIO *wrings his hands and screams.*

DELL' AQUILA (*rushing forward*).

What ho! Torelli!
And you within, you, my lord duke, 'fore all!
I do proclaim you cowards, ruffians, beasts.
Come out, if you be men, and drive my challenge
Back in my throat, if you 've one heart among you!

BERTUCCIO.

You speak to men; they 're fiends.

DELL' AQUILA.

No hope! no hope!
Yes! here 's the Duchess; she 's a woman still —
[*Enter* FRANCESCA *and* GINEVRA, L.

BERTUCCIO.

Madame, and you, too [*To* GINEVRA.], plotting your undoing,
I 've compassed the destruction of my child, —
The daughter that I loved more than my life.
'T was she they seized last night, and she 's in there.
[*Pointing to* C. *door.*

FRANCESCA.

Your child?

BERTUCCIO.

From death, if not wrong worse than death,
You still may save her. Have the doors burst open.
You can command here — next the Duke; if not,
At least [*aside to her*] forbear the poison!

FRANCESCA (*aside to him*).

'T is too late.
The wine was here!

BERTUCCIO.

Then this alone remains.
  [*He rushes up to the door and shouts.*
Come forth, my lords! The Duke's life — all your lives
Hang by a thread! Come forth — all! For your lives!
  [TORELLI, ASCOLTI, *and* ORDELAFFI *appear at the door.*
Your wine is poisoned!

TORELLI.

Ha! Who did the deed?

BERTUCCIO.

I! Drink not — for your lives!
  [*They are rushing upon him, drawing their swords.*

FRANCESCA.

He lies! 'T was I!
  [*A shriek is heard within.*

BERTUCCIO.

My child! my child!

TORELLI (*who has turned back at the sound, flinging the
door wide open*).

Look to the Duke, my lords!

92   THE FOOL'S REVENGE.

[*As the doors are flung open, the interior of the inner room is seen with* THE DUKE *senseless on his seat, and* FIORDELISA *lying at his feet.* TORELLI, ASCOLTI, *and* ORDELAFFI *support* THE DUKE. BERTUCCIO *and* DELL' AQUILA *rush up to* FIORDELISA.

BERTUCCIO.

Too late! too late!

TORELLI.
He's dead!

FRANCESCA.
Before all men,
I'll answer this!

BERTUCCIO.
Before Heaven's judgment seat,
How shall I answer *this?*   [*Pointing to* FIORDELISA
[DELL' AQUILA *has brought* FIORDELISA *forward.* BERTUCCIO *takes her in his arms.*
Dead — dead — my bird!
My lily flower! Gone to thy last account,
All sinless as thou wert. My fool's revenge
Ends but in this! Cold! cold!
[*Putting his hand on her heart.*]   Ha! Yes! a beat!
[*Putting his lips to her mouth.*
A breath! A full deep breath!
She lives! she lives!
Say, some of you, *she* drank not, and I'll bless
The man that says so, — yea, so pray for him
As saints ne'er prayed! She breathes still! Hark! hark!

FIORDELISA (*faintly*).
Father!

TORELLI.

She never drank! Thou hast her pure as when
She kissed thy lips last night!

BERTUCCIO.

Oh, bless you, bless you!
She lives — lives — lives! Leave us to pray together.

TORELLI (*to* FRANCESCA).

Madame, you are our prisoner: the Duke
Lies foully murdered.

FRANCESCA.

Ha! what call you "foully"?
Who but myself can estimate my wrongs?
For those who stand, like him, past reach of justice,
Vengeance takes Justice's sharp sword.

BERTUCCIO.

No, no!
Vengeance is hellish! Justice is from heaven!
Look, Guido Malatesta, I am he
Whose wife, long years ago, *you* stole from him:
I am Antonio Bordiga!

MALATESTA.

You?

BERTUCCIO.

I thirsted for revenge; for that I wrought
Upon the Duke to carry off *your* wife, —
Your innocent Ginevra. Seeking that,
See to what verge of terrible disaster
I've brought my own dear daughter! — seeking that,
I've compassed the Duke's death, whose blood must lie
Still on my head!

FRANCESCA (*proudly*).
                    I take it upon mine!
My father, Giovanni Bentivoglio,
Stands at your gates, in arms! Let who will, question
Francesca Bentivoglio of this deed.

FIORDELISA.
Father, let's pray for her!

BERTUCCIO.
                    For her — for me!
We need it both! Ah, thou said'st well, my child!
Vengeance is not man's attribute, but Heaven's!
I have usurped it.   [*Hiding his face in her bosom*
        Pray — oh, pray for me!

THE END.

LUCRETIA BORGIA

DRAMATIS PERSONÆ.

Don Alphonso d'Este, *Duke of Ferrara.*
Gennaro, *a young soldier of fortune.*
Gubetta, *the poisoner, under the assumed name of the Count de Belverana, a Spaniard.*
Maffio Orsini,
Jeppo Liveretto,
Don Apostolo Gazello, } *Cavaliers of Venice.*
Oloferno Vetillozzo,
Ascanio Petrucca,
Rustighello, *an officer and spy of the Duke's.*
Astolfo, *a servant of the Duchess.*
Baptiste, *Captain of the Guard.*
Pietro.
Lucretia Borgia, *Duchess of Ferrara.*
Princess Negroni.

Monks, Maskers, Lords, Pages, Ladies, etc.

LUCRETIA BORGIA.

ACT I.

SCENE.— *The palace of Barbarigo, at Venice, splendidly illuminated. Grand entrance, with three steps to ascend. A terrace in front, extending from the first wing to the* U. E. *The terrace is festooned with flowers, etc Back is a magnificent view of Venice by moonlight, with the canal of Jucca in front, with handsome gondolas passing and re-passing, from which music is heard, gay and sad alternately, which gradually dies away in the distance.*

Time, night. A carnival. Maskers of all kinds pass and repass to appropriate music Several of the maskers come forward and perform an appropriate dance, and exeunt L. *and* R. U. E.

Enter, L. U. E., GENNARO, MAFFIO ORSINI, DON APOSTOLO GAZELLA, ASCANIO PETRUCCA, OLOFERNO VITELLOZZO, JEPPO LIVERETTO, *come down, and* GUBETTA, *who rather conceals himself from observation, up stage,* L. 2 E. *All have masks in their hands, and all very richly dressed.*

JEPPO.

Now, signors, I am best acquainted with this story.

MAFFIO.

Well, then, give us the full particulars.

OLOFERNO.

There never was a tale more full of horror! There never was a deed more black and damning!

ASCANIO.

Ay, a dark and bloody deed, perpetrated by some malicious demon who revels in blood and crime.

JEPPO.

I know all the particulars, gentlemen; I have them from his Excellency, my cousin, the Cardinal Carriale. You all know the Cardinal Carriale, who —

GENNARO (*throwing himself on a bench*, R., *and yawning*).

Ah, me! I see how it is: Jeppo is going to tell us one of his long stories. Good-bye: I can't stand it; I am already sufficiently worn out.

MAFFIO.

These things, Gennaro, are of too trifling and domestic a nature for your bold and daring spirit. You have no kindred, no father or mother, to whose safety you must look. We have. You are the child of chance; but that you are *noble*, your look, your words, your conduct fully proves, and stamp your greatness on your brow.

GENNARO (*yawning*).

Thank you, worthy friend.

MAFFIO.

But still you cannot claim a right to these **honours yet.**

GENNARO (*starting up*).

Maffio, I make no boast of the purity of my blood, of the nobleness of my rank, or of claims to honours, only as I win them. God is the only parent I have ever known; and the proudest potentate that ever reared his haughty crest to awe us into reverence by his birth and rank can vaunt no higher lineage, or feel more noble than I do now, when I acknowledge that to Him alone I address the holy name of Father!

MAFFIO.

Believe me, I meant not offence. We are brothers in arms. You saved my life at Romana; and we have sworn to aid each other in war and in love, and to revenge each other's wrongs, when required. Our very fates are allied; for, by the predictions of an astrologer, all of us, friends and companions in arms, now together here, are doomed to perish on the self-same day. You say truly, no earthly parent has yet called you son. What, then, are the histories of families to you, who have none? We have an interest in these secret murders: our fathers, mothers, and relatives are concerned. No one of us, except yourself, but has felt the deadly malice of this invisible fiend in the death of some near relative. Our hearts have quivered from the secret stabs of these midnight murderers.

GENNARO (*giving his hand*).

My friend, pardon my ill-timed rashness.

MAFFIO.

From my heart. Come, Jeppo, tell us what you know.

GENNARO (*throwing himself again on bench*, R., *in a sleeping position*).

Pray wake me when Jeppo finishes his story.

JEPPO.

Well, well, fear not our care. And now for my story, which, on my life, is a marvellous one. It was in the year 1480 —

GUBETTA (L., *against column*).

Ninety-seven.

JEPPO.

Ninety-seven! Yes, yes, you are right. In the year 1497, on a certain Sunday —

GUBETTA.

Friday.

JEPPO.

Well, Friday, in November —

GUBETTA.

December.

JEPPO.

Well, you may be right, Count, but it does not matter; November or December, it is all the same. But on a certain Friday night, a waterman of the Tiber, who was sleeping in his boat just below the church Santo Hieronimo, at Ripetta, was awakened by the tramp of footsteps, and raising his head, he perceived through the mists of the night (or, rather, *morning*, I should say, for it was two hours past midnight) two men coming down the street on the left of the church, who walked cautiously about, hither and thither, along the quay. In a few moments two others appeared on the street at the right of the church, who, at a signal from the first, advanced to the river; these were joined by three others, one of whom was mounted on a large white horse, and attended by a comrade on either side, — making, in all, seven men.

GENNARO.

What! the *white horse* made the seventh *man*, Jeppo?

JEPPO.

The quay was silent and deserted. The houses around were shrouded in gloom and darkness, save one, from which gleamed a lonely light. The seven men and the white horse drew nigh to the water's edge, and then the boatman, to his horror and surprise, distinctly perceived a corpse hanging across the pommel of the saddle. Two of the men watched at the corners of the streets, while the others hastily disencumbered the horse of its burden, and, with a violent swing, committed the body to the stream. The man upon the horse then asked, "Is all safe?" to which one of the men replied, "Yes, yes, my lord; no fear of that." They then departed, taking the road to Saint Jacques. This is the boatman's story.

MAFFIO.

Mysterious, indeed! Doubtless a man of rank who had been murdered, and the rider was the assassin.

GUBETTA (*down* L.).

Mysterious, indeed! for on that white horse were two brothers!

JEPPO.

You are right, De Belverana. The horseman was no other than Cæsar Borgia, and the corpse was that of his only brother, John Borgia!

MAFFIO.

A house of demons is that of Borgia. But tell us, Jeppo, why a brother thus assassinated his brother.

JEPPO.

That is almost too horrible to repeat. I cannot tell you now; this is nor time nor place.

GUBETTA (*crossing to* MAFFIO, C.).

I will tell you, signor. Cæsar Borgia, Cardinal of Valence, assassinated John Borgia, Duke of Candia, his brother, with his own hand, at his own altar, because they both loved the same woman.

MAFFIO.

And the woman? Who was the woman?

GUBETTA.

Their cousin. She yet lives, and her name is —

JEPPO.

Enough, enough, Belverana! Do not insult our ears even with the name of that fiend in an angel's form. There is not one of us but has experienced the effects of her infernal power.

MAFFIO.

Methinks I have heard of a child connected with this affair. Is it not so?

JEPPO.

Yes, there was a child, and I have heard his father named.

GUBETTA.

Yes; John Borgia.

MAFFIO.

The child, if living, would be now a man.

OLOFERNO.

Ay, but he has disappeared long since; and whether Cæsar Borgia conceals him from the mother, or the mother from him, no one can tell.

APOSTOLO.

She does wisely, if it be the mother; for this Cæsar Borgia, since he has become Duke of Valence, has slain besides his brother John, his two nephews, sons of Godfrey Borgia, and his cousin the cardinal, Francois Borgia, and has even attempted the life of the Pope. He riots in human blood!

JEPPO.

He aims to become the sole male of the name, and then his wealth would be enormous.

GUBETTA.

That cousin, whom you [*to* JEPPO] are so loath to name, made a secret pilgrimage to the nunnery of St. Sixtus, at the time of the assassination of John Borgia, and secluded herself for many months, no one exactly knowing why.

JEPPO.

I have heard a cause assigned. It was to separate herself from her second husband, John Sforza.

MAFFIO.

What was the boatman's name who saw the act related by you? Know you who he was?

JEPPO.

I do not know.

GUBETTA.

His name was Georgio Schiavone; his business was to trade in provisions and fuel down the Tiber, to Ripetta. He is dead, — died some time since; died *rather* suddenly, some say by poison. It is very likely.

[*Crosses to* R., *and goes up the stage.*

MAFFIO (*in a low tone, to his companions*).

This Spaniard knows more of our affairs than we do ourselves. 'T is strange.

ASCANIO (*low, to* MAFFIO).

I distrust him, as well as yourself. Say nothing, but let us keep an eye upon his movements. Despite that smooth tongue of his, there is danger in him, or I greatly err.

JEPPO.

Ah, gentlemen, what an age we live in! What with war, pestilence, love, intrigue, murder, poison, and the Borgias, show me the man in Italy sure of life for a single day.

APOSTOLO.

Well, comrades, we are, as you are doubtless aware, all attached to the embassy, which the republic of Venice sends to the Duke of Ferrara, to congratulate him on the recapture of Rimni, upon the Maltesta. When do we leave Venice?

OLOFERNO.

The day after to-morrow, certain. The two ambassadors are already appointed, — the Senator Tripolo, and Grimani, the captain of the galleys.

ASCANIO.

Does Captain Gennaro accompany us?

MAFFIO.

Yes, if *I* do. We never separate; we are more than brothers in heart.

ASCANIO (*in a low voice*).

Gentlemen, one word — an important suggestion. For the present, let none of us drink *Spanish* wine.
[*Looking towards* GUBETTA.

JEPPO.

I have another important word: Have you taken care to see that we have any other wine? I have no partiality for Spain; but if the choice is between Spanish wine or no wine at all, I shall embrace Spain decidedly.

MAFFIO.

Let us in. Halloa, Gennaro! Faith! Jeppo, your story had its effect; he sleeps soundly.

JEPPO.

Let him sleep, then. I'll drink his share with my own, for I am devilish thirsty.

[*Exeunt all*, R. U. E., *except* GUBETTA.

GUBETTA (*comes forward*, L. C.).

"This Spaniard knows more of our affairs than we do ourselves," said they. I heard their words, low as they spoke them. Ha, ha, ha! They are right; I *do* know more than they themselves; but Donna Lucretia knows more than I, and my Lord of Valentenois knows more than Donna Lucretia; the devil knows more than my Lord of Valentenois, and Pope Alexander the Sixth knows more, I believe, than the devil himself! [*Looks on* GENNARO.] How these young men sleep! [*Goes down to* L. H. *corner and leans against a pillar.*] Ha! she comes!
[*Enter* LUCRETIA, L. U. E., *magnificently dressed, with her face masked. She looks hurriedly round, does not see* GUBETTA, *approaches* GENNARO, *and gazes fondly and earnestly on his face for some moments, then speaks.*

LUCRETIA.

He sleeps! The *fête* has wearied him! How beautiful! That pale forehead, those jetty locks, those long silken lashes, those proud lips, that noble form! [*Looking up, starts on seeing* GUBETTA, L. LUCRETIA *goes down* C.]
Ha, Gubetta!

GUBETTA (L. C.).

Hush! [*Looking warily round.*] Speak lower, if you please, signora. I am not known as Gubetta here, but as the Count of Belverana, a Castilian noble. And you, madame, do not forget that you are the Countess of Pontequadrato, a Neapolitan lady. We must appear as strangers to each other; such was your Highness's command. Remember, you are not in Ferrara, but in Venice!

LUCRETIA (R. C.).

Right; you are quite right. But there are none within sound of our voices now, save this young soldier, who calmly and soundly sleeps. I wish a moment's converse. [*About to remove mask.*

GUBETTA.

Might I presume to urge your Highness *not* to remove your mask. Some one will recognize you.

LUCRETIA.

Well, and if I *am* recognized, what then? What have I to fear? Let him who makes the discovery tremble he has most cause.

GUBETTA.

We are in Venice, signora, where you have many foes, and they are free! The Republic will guard your person from violence, but it cannot shield you from insult.

LUCRETIA (*sadly*).

True; alas, too true! My very name excites horror, wherever heard.

GUBETTA.

Besides, it is the middle of the carnival, and the city is filled with Romans, Neapolitans, Tuscans, Genoese, Lombards, Romagnols, — Italians of all Italy.

LUCRETIA (*mournfully*).

And all Italy hates me! Ah, me! how sad my fate! But it must not, shall not longer be. I was not born to be the thing I have been and am; and I realize it now.

LUCRETIA (L.).

Gubetta, my old friend, my faithful accomplice, do you not feel a desire to change this kind of life? Have you no wish to be blessed? We two have drawn down curses which, like a mountain's crushing weight, now press upon my heart. Have you not had enough of crime?

GUBETTA (*coolly*).

I perceive plainly that you are about becoming the most virtuous lady in Italy!

LUCRETIA.

Are not our names the synonymes of death, of murder? And does not that sometimes trouble you, as it does me?

GUBETTA.

Not at all, lady. Often, as I pass through the streets of Spoleto or Ferrara, I catch the suppressed execrations of the citizens near me. "There goes Gubetta!" "Gubetta!" cries a second, "the poisoner!" "Gubetta, poniard! Gubetta, gibbet!" exclaims a third; and "Cutthroat! assassin!" with other delicate and complimentary terms pass around; while others, who dare not wag their vile tongues, speak quite as emphatically with their eyes. But what care I for this? I laugh at them, and with a look can make even the boldest tremble. It is my reputation, and as useful to me in my calling as is bravery to a soldier, or devotion to priest.

LUCRETIA.

But see you not that this reputation might excite *hatred* and *horror* in some neart where you might wish for *love?*

GUBETTA.

There are but few in the world whom one *can* love, and they are not always those whom one *should* love.

LUCRETIA.

Gubetta, Gubetta, be silent; you do not comprehend this heart. There is even now in Italy, this fated Italy, *one* pure and noble heart — a heart throbbing with high and holy feelings, brave, noble, daring, though of unknown origin — for whom (God knows its truth!) I would resign all, — life, fame, everything! Oh, to inspire his breast with one gleam of tenderness, one ray of love for me, — a miserable, guilty woman; hated, abhorred, cursed of man and spurned by Heaven; a very *slave*, though the proud mistress of thousands! Oh, could I but hope one day to feel that pure heart throb free and joyously against my own, I would welcome torture, chains, or death to win it! Do you now comprehend me? Can you *now* conceive my anxiety to efface the past, to remove the plague-spot from my name, and in place of the infamy which all Italy now associates with my character, win one of penitence, virtue, and glory?

[LUCRETIA *crosses to* R.

GUBETTA (L.).

Madame! madame! upon what strange herb has your Highness trodden to-day, thus to change your very nature? 'T is droll, in sooth!

LUCRETIA.

Beware! beware, sir! Jest not with me! This is no new fancy; it is not evanescent. But when a weak mortal is hurried on in a current of crime, it is not easy for her to stop when and where she would. Two spirits have for years been struggling here, within this bosom, a good and an evil one. God grant the good one triumph at last!

[*She crosses to* L., *turns up stage, and down again.*

GUBETTA.

All is now explained. All is now clear that before puzzled me. One month ago your Highness left your husband, my Lord Don Alphonso D'Este, with an apparent intention of visiting Spoleto; but under a Neapolitan name you came direct to Venice, and I, your faithful servitor, am directed to take the garb and name of a Spaniard; to this is added a strict injunction neither to speak *to* nor *of* you, or give sign of recognition, should we meet. You visit *fêtes*, operas, balls, and, availing yourself of the privilege of the carnival, go ever masked, while it is but seldom you speak to *any* one, and but a word at a time even to *me*, and that hurriedly and in secret. And now, lo! all this mummery ends in a sermon! A homily, madame, — from *you* to *me!* Is't not strange? You have changed name, dress, rank, residence, bearing, and now it seems your very *nature* is also changed. This is carrying the carnival to an extreme!

[*Crossing to* L.

LUCRETIA (*on his right. She grasps his arm, and draws him towards* GENNARO, *and points to him*).

Do you see that youth?

GUBETTA (L. C.).

He is no stranger to me! He sleeps soundly now, but could sleep still sounder.

LUCRETIA (C.).

Is he not strangely beautiful?

GUBETTA.

He looks well enough for a soldier, and would look better were his eyes not closed. A face like that without eyes is like a palace without windows. [*They come down.*

LUCRETIA (R.).

Ah, you cannot dream, Gubetta, how tenderly I love him!

GUBETTA (L.).

No; that is a *dream* better suited for your royal husband! But your Highness loses time. That young soldier is reported to be in love with a fair young girl called Fiametta.

LUCRETIA (*eagerly*).

And the girl — does she return his love? Speak!

GUBETTA.

Most truly, it is said.

LUCRETIA.

Thank Heaven! Oh, how I pray for his happiness!
[*She goes up to* GENNARO.

GUBETTA.

Stranger still! Another change! I imagined those who loved to be jealous, and I never had cause to consider your Highness an exception to the rule, to say the least.

LUCRETIA (*gazing on* GENNARO).

What a noble figure! and his countenance, so proud, and yet so melancholy! Leave me, Gubetta.

GUBETTA (*crossing to* R.).

I obey your Highness's wishes. She's metamorphosed so strangely that I scarcely know her; and it will puzzle even her holy father the Pope, or his own brother the devil, to recognize her now, I fancy!

[*Exit* GUBETTA, R. 1 E. LUCRETIA *remains gazing a moment; then, perceiving the absence of* GUBETTA, *she looks around to see if she is alone, then speaks.*

LUCRETIA.

This, then, is he. At last I am so blest as to be permitted to gaze on his dear face without peril. Dear — oh, how dear thou art to me!

[*Pause. Enter* DUKE D'ESTE, L. U. E., *accompanied by* RUSTIGHELLO, *both masked and cloaked. They watch her motions, unseen by her.*

Oh, Heaven! spare me the anguish of ever being scorned or hated by him, for thou knowest he is all under heaven that I love! I dare not remove my mask, yet I must wipe away these flowing tears.

[*She takes off her mask, kisses* GENNARO'S *hand, and bends over him; then kneeling, clasps her hands as if in prayer.*

DUKE D'ESTE (*at back* L. U. E.).

That is sufficient. My visit to Venice was to satisfy myself of her infidelity, and I have this night beheld enough to convince me that my suspicions are just. I will now return to Ferrara. That young man is her lover! Who is he, Rustighello?

RUSTIGHELLO.

He is called Captain Gennaro, a soldier of fortune, brave and generous; a man, too, without parents or kin, so far as *he* knows. He is at present in the service of the republic of Venice.

DUKE D'ESTE.

He must be brought to Ferrara.

RUSTIGHELLO.

He will proceed there of his own accord the day after to-morrow, with several of his comrades, who are members of the embassy of Tripolo and Grimani.

DUKE D'ESTE.

'T is well, 't is well; he falls easily into the toils. We can now return. [*Exeunt* D'ESTE *and* RUSTIGHELLO, L. U. E.

LUCRETIA.

Oh, Heaven! may there be as much of happiness in store for him as there has been of misery endured by me! [*She rises, looks anxiously round, kneels, and bends over* GENNARO, *parts the hair from his forehead, and fondly presses her lips to it.* GENNARO *starts and grasps her hand before she can rise, and partly rising, exclaims:*

GENNARO.

A woman! a kiss! by my faith, an adventure! [*They come down stage.*] Happy indeed must those slumbers be which beauty guards. On my honour, were you a queen and I a poet this would be an adventure for Alain Chartier, the troubadour of Provence. You have the grace, the bearing of a queen, but I, alas! am no poet; I am but a soldier.

LUCRETIA (L. C., *with dignity*).

Captain Gennaro, leave me, leave me. Some one approaches. In Heaven's name, do not — do not follow!

GENNARO (C.).

Any command but that, and I am your slave.

LUCRETIA (L. C.).

Do not let your wild companions see me, I entreat; and as you hope to see me more, follow me not now.
[*Exit*, L. 2 E.

GENNARO.

"As I hope to see her more," I'll not lose sight of her now. [*Exit* GENNARO, *following*, L. 2 E.
[*Enter* JEPPO, R. U. E., *as they exeunt. Catches a glimpse of them.*

JEPPO.

Halloa! Gennaro! What form is that which he pursues? Can it be she? It is — it is, by heavens! *That* woman at Venice! What does she here? [*Enter* MAFFIO. R. U. E.] Ha, Maffio!

MAFFIO (*down* R. C.).

How now? What is the matter?

JEPPO (L. C.).

She is here, — that woman of whom we were speaking! she that —

MAFFIO.

Ha! are you sure?

JEPPO.

Quite; as I am that this is the palace of Barbarigo, and not that of Labia.

MAFFIO.

She has an affair of gallantry with Gennaro, then! He must be saved. It is imperiously necessary to draw my brother from the spider's web which that dangerous woman is weaving round him. Quick! let us seek and inform our friends. [*Exeunt*, R. U. E.
[*Gondolas pass at back; music plays from them. Reenter* GENNARO, *holding the hand of* LUCRETIA, L. 3 E. *She is now closely masked again.*

LUCRETIA (R.).

The terrace is now deserted, and I can unmask with safety. I wish you to see my face, Gennaro. [*Unmasks.*

GENNARO (L., *with rapture*).

Beautiful! Ah, signora, you are *very* beautiful!

LUCRETIA.

Look, Gennaro, and look earnestly; then tell me you do not regard my features with horror.

GENNARO.

Horror, lady? On the contrary, my heart involuntarily draws me towards you.

[*Attempts to clasp her. She avoids him.*

LUCRETIA.

Tell me, — oh, tell me truly! — could you *love* me?

GENNARO.

Why should I not love you, beautiful as thou art? But, frankly, my heart is not my own; I love another.

LUCRETIA.

I know who she is, — the fair Fiametta.

GENNARO.

No, lady; oh, no!

LUCRETIA.

Ah! who, then?

GENNARO.

My mother.

LUCRETIA.

Your mother! your mother! Can it be that you love *her* above all others?

GENNARO.

Ay, 't is true; next my God, I adore my mother! And yet I have never seen her face, nor heard her voice, nor felt her soft embrace, nor the warmth of her holy kiss upon my lips. How strange is the feeling that impels me towards you, and makes me speak of that which I never yet imparted even to my foster brother, Maffio Orsini! But it seems as if we had met before — I know not when or where. It is as a dream to me. But listen to me, lady. Of my origin I nothing know. I was reared to the age of seven years by a fisherman of Calabria, whom I had ever looked upon as my father. It was at that period he informed me he was not my sire, — that he could not claim that sacred title. Some time after this, a cavalier, with visor closed, brought me a letter, and then, without disclosing his face or name, departed. That letter was from my mother. Ah, how full of love and tenderness was that letter! It apprised me that I was of noble birth, of ancient family, but no more. She said that she herself was unhappy. Alas, my dear mother!

LUCRETIA (*with great emotion*).

Dear, dear Gennaro!

GENNARO.

Since that day I have been an adventurer, because, being noble by birth, I wished to make myself truly so by my sword. I have roved over all Italy, to discover the secret of my birth, but in vain. Yet, no matter where I am, the first of every month the same messenger brings me a letter from my mother, receives my answer, and departs. We cannot even converse together, for he is deaf and dumb.

LUCRETIA.

And you know nothing of your family?

GENNARO.

I only know I have a mother that loves me, and is herself unhappy.

LUCRETIA.

And her letters, what have you done with *them ?*

GENNARO.

Here! [*Laying his hand upon his breast.*] Here I have them, next my heart! The letters of my mother are the only breastplate I ever wear. Here is her last letter, lady.

[GENNARO *takes a letter from his bosom, kisses it and hands it to* LUCRETIA. *She opens and reads it.*

LUCRETIA (*reads*).

"Seek not to know me, my dear Gennaro, until the day which I shall appoint. I am ever surrounded by those who would destroy me, as they have your poor father. The secret of your birth, my child, must for the present be confined to myself. I fear your daring spirit would start forth and blazon to the world an origin so illustrious as yours. You cannot understand the perils by which you are surrounded. Oh, be content, then, for a little time, to know that you have a mother who adores you, and who watches night and day, unceasingly, over your safety. The time will come, dearest, when you may, without danger, know all ; until then, as you regard your own life, and the life of her who gave you existence, seek not to know more. My son, my own Gennaro, — *adieu!* My heart beats wildly when I think of thee ! my eyes fill with unrestrained tears of tenderness, and my hand falters as I trace these lines for thy dear eyes to gaze upon, while language fails to express the depth, the fathomless depth, of my love for —"

[*She pauses, overcome with emotion, hands the letter back to him, which he again kisses, and places in his bosom.*

GENNARO.

Ah, madame, how tenderly you have read my poor mother's words! You weep, too. Bless you, bless you, lady, for this kind sympathy. You can understand now why I do not yield myself up to pleasure, like my gay comrades. It is because my heart is always full; one thought alone possesses it, — *my mother !* Give me her — to console, to avenge, to serve — and then I can think of love. I am a soldier of fortune, it is true, but I fight no cause but a just one, for I live in the faith and cheering hope of one day laying at my mother's feet a sword bright, unsullied by a single breath. I have ever refused the princely offers proffered me to enter the service of the infamous Lucretia Borgia, but —

LUCRETIA.

Gennaro, Gennaro, hold! You know not what you say. Oh, you should pity the bad, though you condemn their deeds.

GENNARO.

Should we, then, pity those who are themselves so pitiless? But let us speak no more of her. I have told you *my* history; tell me, lady, who *you* are.

LUCRETIA.

An unhappy woman who loves you purely, truly holily.

GENNARO.

And your name, lady?

LUCRETIA.

Ask me no more now; I must not, dare not answer.

MAFFIO (*outside*, R. U. E.).

Nay, Jeppo, follow me; I insist.

LUCRETIA (*crossing to* L. H.).

Great Heaven! what is this? I cannot avoid them; it is too late!

GENNARO.

Fear not, lady; I will defend you with my life.

[*She hastily resumes her mask; then enter*, R. 3 E., MAFFIO, JEPPO, ASCANIO, OLOFERNO, APOSTOLO, *Attendants with torches, Lords, Ladies, pages, etc., as from the palace within.* MAFFIO *and friends range down on* R., LUCRETIA, L., GENNARO, L. C. *Others group above and around, intently observing all.*

MAFFIO.

Gennaro, know you to whom you are speaking of love?

LUCRETIA (*aside*).

Just Heaven, spare him and me!

MAFFIO.

Behold her face, and then — [*Advancing.*

GENNARO (*drawing his sword*).

Maffio Orsini, stand back! You are my friend; you are all friends of mine; but, by heaven! who touches that mask, or lays finger upon this lady, save in kindness, dies. Be she what she may, she is a woman, and my sword and life are pledged to her defence.

MAFFIO.

We wish not to wrong her. Permit us to introduce ourselves.

GENNARO (*pausing a moment*).

Well, be it so. [*Retires up a little,* C

"KNOW YOU TO WHOM YOU ARE SPEAKING OF LOVE?"

MAFFIO (*crossing to* LUCRETIA).

Madame, I am Maffio Orsini, brother to the Duke of Gravina, whom you caused to be stabbed in his dungeon.

JEPPO (*crossing to her*).

Madame, I am Jeppo Liveretto, brother of Liveretto Vittelli, whom your ruffians strangled while he slept.

ASCANIO (*crossing to her*).

Madame, I am Ascanio Petrucca, cousin of Pandolpho Petrucca, Lord of Sienne, who was assassinated by your order, that you might seize his fair city.

GENNARO (*in* C., *a little up*).

Gracious heavens! what means all this?

OLOFERNO (*crossing to her*).

Madame, I am called Oloferno Vitellozzo, nephew of Iago D'Appiani, whom you poisoned at a *fête*, to pillage his lordly castle of Piombino.

APOSTOLO (*crossing to her*).

Madame, you beheaded Don Francisco Gazella, maternal uncle of Don Alphonse of Arragon, your third husband, whom you caused to be murdered on the grand staircase of St. Peter's. I am cousin of one victim, and son of the other.

[*Each gentleman, after addressing* LUCRETIA, *passes up the stage, and falls down to his former situation on* R., *excepting* JEPPO, *who remains* L. C., *near* GENNARO.

LUCRETIA (L., *aside*).

Oh, patience, patience! Must I bear all this?

LUCRETIA BORGIA.

GENNARO (C.).

In Heaven's name, who is this woman?

MAFFIO (R. C.).

And now that we have proclaimed our names and titles, and stated our claims to your regard, permit us to reveal *your* name.

LUCRETIA.

No, no, no! [*Crossing to* C., *and falling on her knees.*] Have pity! Spare me! Have compassion, though *I* merit none; but oh, do not speak! Plunge me into your deepest dungeon, and proclaim it there! shriek it among howling fiends — anywhere — but not before Gennaro!

MAFFIO (*drawing off her mask*).

Let us see if you can yet blush at your crimes.

[*She starts up.*

GENNARO (*enraged, and drawing his sword*).

Maffio Orsini! thus to insult a woman! No more, but draw!

JEPPO (L. H. *of* GENNARO).

Gennaro [*laying his hand on his arm*], you know not what you do! This woman, for whom you would risk your life, is an assassin and an adulteress!

MAFFIO.

And her name —

LUCRETIA.

Spare me! Oh, spare me this! As *you* hope for mercy, spare me!

MAFFIO.

Her name, I say — 't is a spell to empty hell withal, and people earth with devils! Her name is —

LUCRETIA (*turning to him*).

Gennaro, do not — do not listen! I entreat, on my knees, as thou dost revere thy *mother*, dear Gennaro!
[GENNARO *drops his sword at the word "Mother," and clasps his hands.*

MAFFIO.

Her name is Lucretia Borgia!

GENNARO.

Lucretia Borgia! horror!
[*He casts her from him with horror, while she, with a shriek of despair, starts up, advances towards him a step, and falls fainting at his feet.*

ACT II.

SCENE.— *Grand square in Ferrara. On the R a palace, with a latticed balcony, and a grand escutcheon of stone, and with armorial bearings, over which, in bold relief, on a white surface of marble, is the word "* BORGIA*," in large gold letters. On the L. H. is a handsome edifice, opening upon the Square. Streets beyond, with domes, towers, steeples, etc. A large and small door to palace.*

SCENE I.

Enter from U. D. *of palace,* LUCRETIA *and* GUBETTA.

LUCRETIA (L.).
Is all prepared for the night, Gubetta?

GUBETTA (R.).
All is quite ready, your Highness.

LUCRETIA.
All five of them will be present?

GUBETTA.
They are all invited, madame.

LUCRETIA (*with bitterness*).
They have most cruelly outraged my feelings!

GUBETTA (*coolly*).
I was not present. Did all proclaim your name?

LUCRETIA.

They insulted me, mocked my sufferings, vilified my character, publicly tore off my mask, and exposed my face, denounced my name with every epithet of ignominy, — and all before him, of all others in this wide world; before Gennaro! Let me remember that! [*Crosses to* R.

GUBETTA (L. H.).

Fools, fools, to come to Ferrara, then, I trow! But I forgot they could not do otherwise, having been appointed by the senate members of the embassy, which, by the way, arrived here yesterday.

LUCRETIA.

Anything but that I would have borne. But that he — Gennaro — my life's last hope — he now hates, despises me! And they have caused it all! Let me not forget it! O God, revenge shall yet be mine, be sure it shall! [*Crosses to* L. H.

GUBETTA (R.).

I rejoice to hear it; I shall again be busy; I like it.

LUCRETIA (L.).

My very nature seemed changed; my resolves were pure, my aspirations holy. I could have borne all, ay, all but that, — his hate! They should have wrung my heart, and I would have bowed submissively before Heaven, so *he* had still thought kindly of me. But to poison him against me more deeply than ever! O Heaven! the very thought calls from the centre of my heart, and my swelling brain throbs with anguish, while the dark spirit of despair shrieks in my ear, "Revenge!" and it shall have it! [*Crosses to* R.

GUBETTA (L.).

Good! good! I like this! You are yourself again! Your fantasies of mercy have left you, and you act naturally once more. I am now at ease with your Highness. As fire opposes water; light. darkness; and black differs from white, — so stand *I* opposed to the so-styled good and virtuous.

LUCRETIA (R.).

Did Gennaro come here with the others?

GUBETTA.

He did, your Highness.

LUCRETIA (*sternly*).

Gubetta, on your life, see, I charge you, that no harm comes to him! If a hair of his is touched, if he stands in peril, and you avert it not, beware the waked wrath of Lucretia Borgia! Would, would I could but see him once more!

GUBETTA.

That you can do at any hour. I induced his valet to take that house (*points to* L. H.) for his master. Your balcony commands a view of it, and, concealed from sight, you can see him go in and out as often as you choose to enjoy that ineffable delight.

LUCRETIA.

Nay, I would speak with him.

GUBETTA.

Nothing is easier, signora. Send Astolfo with a message that your Highness, to-day, at a certain hour, would see him at the palace, on business of high import.

LUCRETIA (*thoughtfully*).

Yes, I could do that; but would he come?

GUBETTA.

He could be *caused* to obey. But go in, your Highness, for I momentarily expect them to pass this way. It were better that they saw you not. I will meet them.

LUCRETIA.

They still consider you the Count of Belverana?

GUBETTA.

Ay; I have convinced them on that point past doubt. I have borrowed their money.

LUCRETIA.

Borrowed their money! and why?

GUBETTA.

To have them in my power. Nothing binds friends so fast as money borrowed or lent; and it is so decidedly Spanish, as an air of poverty, while at the same time we seize the devil by the tail.

LUCRETIA.

Silence, sir! This is no time for jests. But see, they are coming down yonder street, and Gennaro is with them. Gubetta, I charge you, guard from harm or danger *Gennaro!* [*Exit* LUCRETIA *into palace*, U. D.

GUBETTA.

Who the devil *is* this Gennaro, in whom she takes such an interest? and what the devil does she design doing with him? It is quite plain I am not in *all* the secrets of this fair lady. It touches my curiosity. In faith, she has not reposed her usual confidence in me in this matter. Madame Lucretia is becoming platonic. Well, I am astonished at nothing. But here are the young bloods of Venice. They are not over wise, to leave the free state of Venice and come to Ferrara after having offended the Duchess of Ferrara. Were *I* they, I should have stayed away. But young people *will* be rash. The throat of a tigress is of all sublunary places that into which they precipitate themselves most eagerly. Well, let the fools have their way.

[*Retires behind a pillar of the balcony.*
[*Enter*, L. U. E., MAFFIO, APOSTOLO, JEPPO, ASCANIO, OLOFERNO, *and* GENNARO. *They converse in a low tone, and with inquietude.*

MAFFIO.

Say what you please, friends, but we are not very safe here in Ferrara, after having insulted the Duchess, Lucretia Borgia.

APOSTOLO.

But what could we do? The signory of Venice appointed us, and their fiat is imperative, were it to exterminate one's own family. There is no disguising it, however, that Lucretia Borgia is to be dreaded, and she is supreme in Ferrara.

JEPPO.

She dare not harm us; we are in the service of the republic of Venice, and form a part of her embassy. Let this duchess touch a hair of our heads, and the doge would instantly declare war; and Ferrara would not willingly rub against Venice now.

MAFFIO.

Ah, you may be stretched at full length in your sepulchre without touching a *hair* of your head. It is *by poison* the Borgia family effect their purposes,—a poison of so subtle a nature that no medicine on earth can remedy. It is sure and deadly, noiseless, and better than the axe or the poniard. These Borgias have poisons which kill in a day, a month, or year, as they please. It is by it they impart a more pleasing flavour to their wines, so that the drinker more eagerly drains his cup, and, with joy and rapture in his face, falls dead. Sometimes a foe of the Borgias falls into a state of melancholy, his skin wrinkles, his eyes sink deep in the head, his hair turns white, the teeth fall out, his knees are weak, and while he breathes, you hear the death-rattle in his throat. Sleep forsakes him; he shivers in the noonday sun with cold, and youth puts on the appearance of old age. He dies, and then it is recollected that he drank a cup of Cypress wine at the palace of a Borgia!

ASCANIO.

This is horrible! It were well that we quit Ferrara. Our ambassadors have an audience of the Duke to-day, and we shall then be at liberty to leave. I would we had never come.

JEPPO.

Well, to-morrow we can go. I am invited to sup with the Princess Negroni, with whom I am almost in love, and I would not fly from the prettiest woman in all Ferrara.

OLOFERNO.

The Princess Negroni? I am invited too!

MAFFIO.

And I!

APOSTOLO.

And I!

ASCANIO.

And I!

GUBETTA.

And so am I, gentlemen.

[*Coming forward from behind pillar.*

JEPPO.

Aha! the Count of Belverana!   [*Shaking his hand.*
Good! we'll all go together, and a merry night we'll make it!

GUBETTA (*crossing to* JEPPO).

May his holiness have you in sacred keeping many years, Signor Jeppo.

MAFFIO (*in a low tone, to* JEPPO).

Let us not go to this feast to-night. I have a presentiment of ill; and, besides, I distrust this amiable count.

JEPPO.

Pooh! he was my father's companion in arms! But do as you please; I shall go.

[LUCRETIA *appears on the balcony,* R., *listening.*

ASCANIO (*to* GENNARO, *who is musing,* L. H.).

Speak! Are you not invited, Captain?

GENNARO.

No; the Princess would not notice a poor soldier like myself. But she would have found me bad company at the best.

MAFFIO (*crossing to* GENNARO).

Ah! I suspect you have a rendezvous *d'amour;* is it not so?

JEPPO.

Apropos! tell us what said the fair Lucretia to you the other evening. She is in love with you, 'tis clear. Masked face, but a naked heart!

MAFFIO.

And, my brother, you have taken lodgings directly opposite to hers. Ah, Gennaro, Gennaro!

JEPPO.

Take care, Gennaro, for they do say the Duke is not a little jealous of his beautiful wife. Come, enlighten us poor devils about her — do!

ALL.

Ay, do! Signor Gennaro in love! Ha, ha, ha!

GENNARO.

Gentlemen, I have borne your raillery thus long, because we are sworn friends; but if you couple my name again with that of the infamous Lucretia Borgia, you will see swords flashing in the sun! I respect you all, but I respect my honour more!

LUCRETIA (*aside*).

Alas! alas! they have accomplished it! He hates my very name!

MAFFIO.

Why, Gennaro, brother, we are only indulging in a little pleasantry, and we have good right to do so when a gallant cavalier wears a lady's colours on his bosom.

GENNARO.

I! What mean you?

MAFFIO (*pointing to his scarf*).

That scarf.

JEPPO.

Yes, my friend, that scarf. Is it not the colours of the Duchess?

GENNARO.

This scarf was sent me by Fiametta Berano, in Venice.

MAFFIO.

You may believe so, if you like, but 't was from the hands of the fair Lucretia, I'll be sworn.

GENNARO.

Gentlemen, I'm in no mood for jesting now. Are you sure of what you say?

JEPPO.

Sure! Why, every child knows the colours of the Duchess; and, to be plain, your own valet was bribed to tell you this tale, as from Fiametta; he acknowledged it to me.

GENNARO.

Damnation! [*Tears off the scarf, and tramples it under foot.*] Thus do I tread upon her gifts, and thus do I scorn the terrible Borgia! [*Crosses to* R. C.

LUCRETIA (*with great feeling, pressing her hands to her forehead*).

'T is past! Farewell all my bright visions of happiness! Oh, farewell to peace! He tramples on my very heart! It is not *him* I blame; but let those who have caused this, and planted in his heart this horror, beware of a greater one! Let them now, if they can, escape from the awakened wrath of the scorned Lucretia Borgia! [*She retires from the balcony.*

MAFFIO.

How bright and beautiful she is — this Lucretia — notwithstanding her fiendish nature! I am told she was not always so.

GENNARO.

Name her not again! I scorn — detest her! Love her, said you? Love the woman who murdered your brother, whose place I now fill in your heart! Let us think only of that! See, here is the accursed palace of luxury, and seat of festering crime, — the home of a Borgia! The mark of infamy which I cannot stamp upon the forehead of this woman I will leave at least on the front of her palace!

[*He leaps on to a stone step, and with his dagger erases the first letter of the word* BORGIA *on the wall, so that there remains but the word* ORGIA.

MAFFIO.

For God's sake, Gennaro, what have you done? Your life is now in deadly peril every coming moment!

GUBETTA (R. *corner*).

Signor, you have but shortened the lady's name by a letter; when next she meets you, she'll shorten your body by a head, at least! Half the city will to-morrow be questioned for that pun, signor.

GENNARO.

Let the other half, then, say it was I, and be you the first!

MAFFIO.

Gentlemen, let us leave this place. I like it not; and have you not observed those two men, who seem to have been watching us?

JEPPO.

I have. They are, no doubt, a couple of amiable cut-throats.

MAFFIO.

Gennaro, as you value the safety of your friends, no more bravado! If you are in peril, I have sworn to share it, remember!

GENNARO.

Your hand, brother. Fear me not. Gentlemen, good-night. [*Exit into house on* L. H.

JEPPO (*going up with the others*).

Good-night. The very devil is in our friend to-night. Gentlemen, pause. A last look! [*All turn round; pointing at the word.*] Orgia! That is indeed a joke!

[*All exeunt,* L. U. E., *laughing, except* GUBETTA.

GUBETTA.

A joke, is it? Ha, ha! I'm a little afraid, my friends, that you'll find it a serious one before the Duchess and myself have got over it. And Gennaro, too! Ha, ha, ha! Good, good! very good! I like that! The lady will not relish such a joke, even from him. I shall soon be wanted, I see plainly. The devil never deserts his friends, and I am a favoured subject. I thank him.

[*Exit into palace through* U. D.

SCENE II.

A street in Ferrara. Enter RUSTIGHELLO, R., *and* ASTOLFO, L. H.

ASTOLFO.
Good-day. What movement brought you this way?

RUSTIGHELLO.
The usual one, I believe.

ASTOLFO.
Well, what are you doing here?

RUSTIGHELLO.
Watching and waiting for you to be gone. And what are you doing?

ASTOLFO.
Watching and waiting for *you* to be gone.

RUSTIGHELLO.
Indeed! Whom are you looking for?

ASTOLFO.
The young Venetian, Captain Gennaro.

RUSTIGHELLO.
And so am I — with an invitation from the Duke.

ASTOLFO.
And I bear an invitation from the Duchess.

RUSTIGHELLO.
What awaits him from the Duchess, think you?

ASTOLFO.

Love, no doubt. What from the Duke?

RUSTIGHELLO.

Death, no doubt.

ASTOLFO.

What's to be done? He can't wait on both these invitations very well at once. He can't be a lover and a corpse at the same time.

RUSTIGHELLO.

Stay, I have an idea how we can settle this. Here's a ducat. I'll toss it up, and let the side which turns up determine which of us shall have the guest. I choose the Duke's head; the cross shall be yours.

ASTOLFO.

So be it. If I lose, I'll tell the Duchess the bird had flown; and if you lose, you must say the same to the Duke.

RUSTIGHELLO.

Certainly. It matters little to me which of us wins; so here goes. I say, "head's up!" [*Tosses up the coin.*

ASTOLFO.

And "head" it is. He is yours, and will die. The man was born to be hanged, it seems. So be it. Fate settles it, not I. There's his lodging. (L. H.). Now I'll return to the Duchess. [*Exit*, R. H.

RUSTIGHELLO.

Now for the Captain! The Duke invites! [*Exit*, L. H

Don Alphonso D'Este.

SCENE III.

[*A splendid apartment in the ducal palace. Hangings of tapestry of Hungarian leather, elaborately stamped with arabesque and grotesque figures of gold, in the style of the fifteenth century (the latter part). A large door in* C., *and two small doors* R. *and* L. H. *The one on* L. H. *is a secret door, and looks like the panelling, until it is opened. On* R. H., *state chair, embroidered with arms of the house of D'Este. On* R. C. *an elegant table, covered with a rich cloth of scarlet, with books, papers, rich inkstand, pens, etc. A Gothic chair beside the table.* DON ALPHONSO D'ESTE, DUKE OF FERRARA, *in splendid attire, in his robe of rank, is discovered at table writing. Enter* RUSTIGHELLO, L. H. D., 1 E.

RUSTIGHELLO.

My lord duke, your first orders are executed. The prisoner is in the palace. I await your further order.

DUKE D'ESTE (*taking a small key from bosom*).

Take this key and go to the Numa Gallery; count all the panels of the wainscot, commencing at the figure of Hercules, till you come to the twenty-third. Search carefully, and in the mouth of one of the painted dragons you will find a small opening. Insert this key, then press upon it, and the panel will turn, as upon pivots. In this secret recess you will find a small salver of gold, and near it a golden flagon, and a flagon of silver, with two enamel cups. Take them, without disturbing their contents in any way, to my private cabinet. I need not warn you not to taste their contents.

RUSTIGHELLO.

Is that all, my lord?

DUKE D'ESTE.

No; when you have executed my order, do you take your station in my cabinet, there (R. D. F.), where you may hear all that passes. If I ring this silver bell, immediately enter with your drawn sword; but if I call you by name, enter with the salver and wine. Go!

[RUSTIGHELLO *bows and exits by the small* D. R. H. *in* F. THE DUKE *rises, paces the chamber with an agitated air a moment, and then throws himself into his chair, and leans his head upon his hands. Enter* ASTOLFO, C. D.

ASTOLFO.

My lady the Duchess demands an audience with your Highness.

DUKE D'ESTE.

We await the Duchess.

[*Exit* ASTOLFO, C. D. *Enter* THE DUCHESS LUCRETIA, C. D., *impetuously*.

LUCRETIA.

My lord duke, some one has mutilated the name of your wife, engraved over the armorial bearings of our house, in front of this palace; some one of your people, I fear it is. This is an indignity too infamous patiently to bear. It has been done in public, in the broad face of day. Do you hear it, sir? I know not the offender's name; but, by the Virgin! I will not tamely tolerate this insult. I would rather a thousand times die by the poniard than have my name made the vile jest, the quibble and sarcasm of the rabble. I demand justice! Can you calmly sit there and hear of this insult to your wife? Or is it because it is not against yourself that you bear it thus? You say you love me; show that you love my fair fame. You are jealous, too; show that it is for my reputation. I demand justice! You are the Duke, and can give it. You are my husband, and *shall* protect me! You have given me your hand, and I now demand the strength of your strong arm.

DUKE D'ESTE (*calmly*).

Madame, what you complain of was known to me.

LUCRETIA.

Known, sir, and the criminal not discovered!

DUKE D'ESTE.

The criminal *is* discovered.

LUCRETIA.

Let him be instantly arrested.

DUKE D'ESTE.

He *is* arrested.

LUCRETIA.

Then why is he not punished?

DUKE D'ESTE.

I awaited your counsel, madame.

LUCRETIA.

I thank you. Where is the miscreant?

DUKE D'ESTE.

Here, in the palace.

LUCRETIA.

Here! He shall be made an example of. It is high treason, my lord. It is fitting that the head which conceives and the hand that executes should be forfeited. I will pass sentence with my own lips.

DUKE D'ESTE.

You shall do so. Baptiste! [*Enter* BAPTISTE, L. H. D., 1 E.] Show in the prisoner.

    [*Exit* BAPTISTE, L. H. D., 1 E. THE DUKE *rises*.

LUCRETIA.

A word yet, my lord. Be this man who he may, — one of your own family, an officer of your household, even a subject of Venice, — swear by your ducal crown he shall not depart alive!

DUKE D'ESTE.

Mark me well. I swear, by my sacred honour and by my ducal crown, he *dies*, be he who he may!

LUCRETIA.

My lord, I am content; now I would see the prisoner.
[*Enter*, L. H. D. 1 E., GENNARO, *disarmed, and four Guards.*
  THE DUKE *sits in state chair*, R. H.

LUCRETIA (*seated in chair*, L. *of table*).

Gennaro! [*With agony.*] My lord, what fatality is this?

    DUKE D'ESTE (*smiling, and in an undertone*).

What! you know this man, then, Lucretia?
[*She gazes a moment on him, then sinks into the chair at table.*

GENNARO.

My lord duke, I am a simple captain in the service of Venice. You have ordered my arrest; I address you with that respect befitting your rank, and ask of what I stand accused.

DUKE D'ESTE.

Signor, the crime of high treason! The family name of our much loved duchess, Lucretia Borgia, has been shamefully mutilated on the façade of our own ducal palace. We seek the criminal.

LUCRETIA (*eagerly*).
It is not he, Alphonso! It is not this young man!

DUKE D'ESTE.
How know you that, Lucretia?

LUCRETIA.
It cannot be. He is of Venice, not of Ferrara. The act was committed this morning, and he was then, I'm told, with one named Fiametta.

GENNARO (L.).
Your pardon. It is not true, your Highness.

DUKE D'ESTE.
You see your Highness has been wrongly informed. Captain, on your honour, are you the man who committed this offence?

LUCRETIA (*rises in terror*).
Air! air! I suffocate! [*Crosses to* L., *and in passing whispers to* GENNARO, *rapidly.*] Oh, say it was not you!

DUKE D'ESTE (*aside*).
She whispered him as she passed!

GENNARO.
Duke Alphonso, the fisherman of Calabria who reared me, taught me this maxim: "Do what you promise, and honestly say what you have done." By acting thus, one may often hazard life, but he preserves his honour. Duke, I am the man!

DUKE D'ESTE.
Madame, you have my oath on my ducal crown!

LUCRETIA (*with effort*).
Guards, retire with your prisoner a moment. My lord, a word with you. [THE DUKE *comes down.*
[*Exeunt* BAPTISTE *and Guards*, D. L. 1 E., *with* GENNARO.

DUKE D'ESTE (R.).
Madame, what would you with me?

LUCRETIA (L.).
It is my will, Alphonso, that this young man should live.

DUKE D'ESTE.
Indeed! how very strange! A few moments since, you demanded, with tears and imprecations, justice against one who had insulted you. You made me pledge my word, — nay, swear an oath, that the offender should die. I did so. You have my oath. He is guilty, by his own confession; and again, mark me, by my soul he dies! You are at liberty to choose the manner of his death; but I have called God to witness an oath, and it shall be sacred.

LUCRETIA (*laughing, and with great tenderness*).
Don Aphonso, I am a true woman, — wayward and capricious, spoiled by foolish indulgence. You know my temper. Let us reason, cordially, tenderly, like man and wife. Be seated.
[LUCRETIA *sits* R. *of table.* THE DUKE *kneels to her on foot-stool on her left.*

DUKE D'ESTE (*with an air of gallantry*).
At your feet. I am ever happy to be here, for you are queen of love. as well as of beauty.

LUCRETIA.

You know I love you, Alphonso. I am cold sometimes, and it is natural to my character; but it does not proceed from want of affection for you. Whenever you have chid me mildly, have I not yielded? and I would do so ever, dear lord!

DUKE D'ESTE.

Nay, I bow to you. My fair wife. [*Putting his arm round her waist.*] You are brilliant as the star of evening, and your bright eyes, soft lips, and angel form would wake an anchorite to passion.

LUCRETIA.

Is it not ridiculous that we should quarrel — we who are seated on the first ducal throne in the world — about a Venetian adventurer, a mere soldier of fortune? We must put him away, and say no more about it. A silly braggart to annoy us thus! Let him depart. I will tell Baptiste to send this Gennaro out of Ferrara instantly, that he may no longer be the cause of discord.

DUKE D'ESTE.

Nay; why such haste? There is time enough.

LUCRETIA.

I wish to have it from our thoughts. Nay, you must let me have this affair my own way.

DUKE D'ESTE.

This must be *my* way Lucretia. The man must die!

LUCRETIA.

Why, what cause have you to wish for this young man's life?

DUKE D'ESTE (*rising*).

My word is given. The oath of a prince is sacred.

LUCRETIA.

That is well enough to tell the people; but between you and me, Alphonso, we know what it is. You gave your oath to Petrucci to render Sienne; you have not done it, nor ought you to do it. The history of nations is full of this.

DUKE D'ESTE (L.).

But, Lucretia, an oath!

LUCRETIA (R.).

Give me no more of such reasoning; I am no fool. Come, give me his life as readily as you gave me his death, unless you have a reason to give instead. You are silent. It is I who am insulted, not you.

DUKE D'ESTE.

That is precisely why I will not accord him grace.

LUCRETIA.

My lord, if you love me, you will no longer deny this trivial boon. Let us be merciful. Mercy, Alphonso, is that quality alone in which man may imitate his Maker.

DUKE D'ESTE.

Mark me, for the last time! I cannot, *will not!* He dies!

LUCRETIA.

"Will not" and "cannot"! Why will you not?

DUKE D'ESTE.

I will tell you why. This adventurer is your lover! [*She starts.*] You sought him in Venice, and met him

LUCRETIA BORGIA.

DUKE D'ESTE.

Do lovers never quarrel? His mode of death, — decide! No answer? Then the sword!

[*About to raise the bell from table.*

LUCRETIA (*seizing his hand*).

Stay! oh, stay!

DUKE D'ESTE.

Will you please to pour out for your lover a glass of Syracuse wine?

LUCRETIA.

Oh, Gennaro!

DUKE D'ESTE.

He must die

LUCRETIA.

Not by the sword! not by the sword! I — I — choose the other mode.

DUKE D'ESTE.

You cannot deceive me! The wine must be poured out from the *gold* flagon! You know its superior qualities; and till he drinks, be sure I leave not your side. Baptiste! [*Enter* BAPTISTE, L. H. D. 1 E.] Bring in your prisoner! [BAPTISTE *exits and re-enters*, L. H. D. 1 E., *with* GENNARO, *guarded, as before.*] Captain Gennaro, we have reason to believe the offence of this morning was the thoughtless folly of youth, rather than malice and design of insult. On this account the Duchess of Ferrara pardons you, on condition that you immediately depart for Venice. You are called brave and generous, and we desire not to deprive the Republic of a single faithful arm now, when Candia and Cyprus are threatened by the Saracen.

GENNARO (L.).

My lord duke, your clemency has my thanks, and doubly so, as I looked not for mercy at your hands. I thank you.

DUKE D'ESTE.

Well, that is past. How like you the service of Venice? On what conditions are you engaged?

GENNARO.

I command fifty mounted men, my lord, whom I feed, clothe, and pay; for which I am allowed two thousand sequins of gold a year.

DUKE D'ESTE.

Would you enter my service if I were to give you four thousand sequins?

GENNARO.

For two years I must still serve the republic of Venice, for which term I am bound.

DUKE D'ESTE.

How "bound," Captain?

GENNARO.

My lord, by oath.

DUKE D'ESTE (*low to* LUCRETIA, *with a smile*).

You hear, madame; even a poor adventurer regards his "oath." [*Aloud to* GENNARO.] Have you any favour to ask, any boon to crave, before you leave Ferrara?

GENNARO.

I have not; but I will mention one thing before I depart, as an equivalent return for the life you have now spared. As your clemency has been freely extended, I name it, but should not have done so otherwise. Your Highness may not have forgotten that at the storming of Faenza, two years since, your brother, the Duke Hercules d'Este, was in deadly peril from two halberdiers of the enemy. His life was saved by a young soldier of Venice.

DUKE D'ESTE (*rising*).

'T is true, and I have sought that brave soldier in vain.

GENNARO.

He now stands before you, Duke!

DUKE D'ESTE.

Ah, is it so, indeed? My gallant captain! [*Comes forward, and grasps his hand.* THE DUCHESS *starts up, and advances,* R. H.; *after a pause, returns to seat.* THE DUKE *observing the joy of* THE DUCHESS *drops* GENNARO'S *hand.*] Will you accept this purse of gold sequins?

GENNARO (L.).

My lord duke, I am pledged to the Republic not to receive gold from any foreign prince. Yet though I may not take it for myself, I will, with your permission, present it to these brave soldiers here, — my guard.

DUKE D'ESTE (C.).

The purse is yours. But you will not refuse to join us in a glass of Syracusan wine? [*Going up to table.*

GENNARO.

Most willingly, my lord.

DUKE D'ESTE (*at table*).

Rustighello! [*He enters,* R. D. F.] The wine! [*He exits.*] And to do honour to the brave soldier who saved my brother's life, the Duchess shall with her own fair hand pour out for you. [GENNARO *bows, and turns to the soldiers, to whom he gives the money. Enter* RUSTIGHELLO, *with the wine,* R. D. F.] 'T is well. [*Aside.*] Lucretia, listen to what I tell this man. [*To* RUSTIGHELLO.] Place yourself near that door; if I ring this bell, enter with your drawn sword. Now go! [*Exit* RUSTIGHELLO, R. D. F.] Captain Gennaro! Madame, pour out for our friend, from the *gold* flagon.

LUCRETIA (*seated* R. *of table. In a low tone to* THE DUKE).

Oh, must it be? Alphonso! husband! think, — he saved your brother's life! *Must* it be so? As there is a heaven above, I swear to you your suspicions are false? Did you but know what a horrible crime you are forcing me to commit, you would pause, my lord, — you would pause!

DUKE D'ESTE (L. *of table, carelessly*).

Take care, Lucretia; do not mistake the flagon. Pray, what may be your age, Captain?

[THE DUKE *fills for himself from the silver flagon, and raises it to his lips.*

GENNARO (L. C.).

Twenty years, your Highness.

[THE DUCHESS *is about to fill from the silver flagon the cup which* GENNARO *holds out as he replies.*

DUKE D'ESTE.

Lucretia, fill from the *gold* flagon, if you please, — or, shall I ring for the servant who waits my order at the door? It would, indeed, have been cruel, Lucretia, to have cut him off from life, from love, from the bright future that is before him, — on the very threshold of manhood, too, only twenty years of age, — from the gay *fêtes*, the masks, and carnivals of Venice, and the fair ones who love him, and whom he doubtless loves, would it not?

LUCRETIA (*aside*).

Oh, heaven! if he would but meet my eye, I might warn him with a glance.

GENNARO.

My lord duke, I value not life; but for the sake of my poor mother, I thank you for preserving it.

LUCRETIA.

Oh, horror! [*Aside. Sinks into chair.*

DUKE D'ESTE.

Your health, Captain Gennaro. May you live a thousand years.

GENNARO.

God bless you, my lord duke. [*Both drink.*

DUKE D'ESTE.

Farewell, Captain; you are free to depart, and I wish you a safe and a speedy journey. I must leave you now. [THE DUKE *rises. Aside, to* LUCRETIA.] I leave you with your lover, Lucretia. He is now all your own,—yours while he lives; and if you choose to share his fate, you are at liberty to be his in death. Thus perish all your paramours, madame! [*Exit,* C. D.

LUCRETIA.

Guards, you may withdraw. [*Exit Guards,* L. 1 E. LUCRETIA *watches them off, then starts up wildly from her seat, goes to* C. D., R. H. D. F., *and* D. L. 1 C; *fastens them; then rushes to* GENNARO, *and exclaims:*] Gennaro, Gennaro, you are poisoned!

GFNNARO.

Poisoned, madame!

LUCRETIA.

Yes, yes, Gennaro. Oh, my God, you are poisoned!

GENNARO.

The wine was poured out by your own hand. True, true, I might have suspected it. You are Lucretia Borgia!

LUCRETIA.

Gennaro, Gennaro, you will drive me mad! Do not, oh, do not *you* reproach me, or my senses will forsake me! Listen to me. The Duke is mad with jealousy, believes you to be my lover, and left me no alternative but to see you poniarded by Rustighello (who is even now there) or pour out for you that wine with my own hands. It is a sure and deadly poison, — a poison the very mention of which makes every Italian turn pale who knows the history of the last twenty years; it is the poison —

GENNARO.

Of the Borgias

LUCRETIA.

Yes, and you have it in your veins! I can and must save you! [*Producing a small and elegant gold phial from her bosom.*] Here, here is an antidote, known but to two persons in the wide world, — my father and myself. Quick! one drop on your lip, and you are saved!
[*She approaches with the phial; he recoils from her, and gazes fixedly upon her face.*

GENNARO.

Madame, is not *this* the poison?

LUCRETIA.

Oh, misery! misery!

GENNARO.

I have not forgotten the fate of the brother of Bajazet. He was persuaded that he was poisoned, and took the proffered antidote; it caused his death.

LUCRETIA.

Great Heaven! must he perish by my hand? Oh, wretched, wretched woman that I am! Gennaro, hear me! [*On her knees.*] By the dread name of Him who readest the hearts of all, by the sacred love you bear your mother, I swear you are poisoned! Drink, drink this, ere I go mad! Your reproaches crush me, warp my reason; but I have but one thought, hope, wish, prayer, — to save you! Curse me, heap on my head your maledictions, crush me with contempt and scorn, but, as you ever hope to know your mother, drink this!

GENNARO.

Madame, I saved the life of the Duke's brother; he is loyal and noble. You I have offended, and I have reason to dread your vengeance.

LUCRETIA.

Gennaro, if to give up my whole life would add one hour to yours; if to spill the last drop of my blood could hinder you from shedding one tear; if by torture I could seat you on a throne, — I would not hesitate, murmur; I would do it, and die happy, too happy, to be your slave! The Duke may soon return; he thinks you already dead; in a few moments it will be too late to save! It is a choice of life or death! Gennaro, drink this, and live!

GENNARO.

Lucretia Borgia, give me the phial! I am a friendless orphan, a lone being on earth. It may be that you speak truly; if not, be sure the God of the fatherless will avenge me. [*He drinks, and hands it to her.*

LUCRETIA (*falls on her knees in thankfulness*).

He's saved! he's saved! thank God, he's saved! [*Rising.*] Now lose not a moment, but mount a fleet steed, and begone! I have already sent one to your house; he waits your coming. Escape to Venice, and Heaven guard you! Have you money?

GENNARO.

I have, madame.

[*She takes him up to secret door,* L. F., *and opens it.*

LUCRETIA.

Stay one instant. Here, take this phial; keep it ever near you, for poison is in every cup! Now fly for your life! Yet one word more, and then farewell forever!

GENNARO.

Speak! I trust you now; I listen.

LUCRETIA (*with great emotion*).

We are parting forever. I had hoped to have seen you during your bright career, — to have marked your rising greatness. It cannot be; it puts your life in peril. We are parting, then, forever in this life! Gennaro, Gennaro, one word; have you not one kind word for me at parting, — only one, for the being who loves you better than her own soul; only one, ere we separate for eternity?

GENNARO.

You have saved my life, you say. I will believe it; I will forget all I ever heard, — ay, I will leave you with Heaven's blessing, if you but swear, by all that is sacred (by my own life, since I am dear to you), that your crimes have not caused misery to my dear but unknown mother.

LUCRETIA.

Gennaro, all I ever utter to you is truth; I will **not** be false in word or deed to you, and I cannot swear that oath

LUCRETIA BORGIA. 155

GENNARO.

Oh, heavens! my mother! This, then, is the being who caused you a life of misery!

LUCRETIA.

Gennaro, hold! No; I am —

GENNARO.

You have avowed it! Adieu, Lucretia Borgia! adieu forever! Be thou accursed! [*Exit*, L. D. F.

LUCRETIA.

And be thou blessed forever!
[*Noise*, C. D. *She rushes up to* L. D. F., *closes the door, and comes down* R., *just as* THE DUKE *bursts open* C. D., *and rushes in.*

DUKE D'ESTE (*comes down* L.).

Now, where is Gennaro, madame?

LUCRETIA.

Seek him.

DUKE D'ESTE.

Guards! [*Rushes to* L. D. 1 E.; *finds it fast.*] Ah, closed! Rustighello! [*Rushes up to* R. D. F.] All closed! Where, where is Gennaro?

LUCRETIA.

With a drug I preserved his life! He is now on his road to Venice, and out of your power forever! Ha, ha, ha! *I* triumph now! He's safe! he's safe! thank God, he's safe! [*Falls fainting on the stage.*

DUKE D'ESTE.

Escaped! Furies seize thee! [*Rusnes out*, C. D.

ACT III.

SCENE. — *A magnificent chamber in the Negroni Palace. On the* R. *a* D. *In* C., *very large curtain, size of half the flat, to draw aside each way. Splendid chandeliers and candelabra. Magnificent banquet, with wines, fruit, and all kinds of eatables, served up in the costly style of the fifteenth century. Pages attending. Music, soft, but gay, is heard as the curtain rises. All the guests are seated,* ASCANIO, OLOFERNO, APOSTOLO, JEPPO, *and* GUBETTA, *and several ladies, elegantly dressed. At the head of the table is the* PRINCESS NEGRONI.

OLOFERNO.

Here's the wine of Xeres! Xeres de la Frontera is a city of Paradise.

JEPPO.

Bravo, Signor Oloferno! you improve. But this wine is of great power and unequalled flavour. The last time we cavaliers drank together, 't was in Venice, at the palace of his serene Highness, Doge Barbarigo; now we are at Ferrara, and in the palace of the divine Princess of Negroni. We drink to your health and your beauty.
[*All rise, and raising their glasses, bow to her. Enter,* R. D. 1 E., MAFFIO *and* GENNARO, *the latter very reluctantly.*

MAFFIO.

Why, brother, what unaccountable dullness is this? and why am I obliged to go to your lodgings ere I can get you here? Egad! 't was devilish lucky I went when I did, or you would have escaped us. When I saw your horse at the door I suspected your trick, my friend.

GENNARO.

I know not why I have consented to delay my departure for Venice, and I regret that I have done so, even now. Had you not convinced me that I had been the dupe of that artful woman, I should have been already far on my way.

MAFFIO.

Ha, ha, ha! it was excellent, i' faith! The Duke poisons you, and the Duchess gives you a counter poison! Why, what a farce! The fair Lucretia is desperately in love, and she pretends to save your life, so that from gratitude you may at last reciprocate her regard.

GENNARO (R.).

But the Duke?

MAFFIO (L.).

Oh, he's a good-natured, easy fellow, a little jealous of his fair rib, — and he has cause, I fear, you rogue! — but utterly incapable of poisoning. Besides, you saved his brother's life.

GENNARO.

But why is the Duchess so anxious for my absence from Ferrara, if, as you say, she loves me?

MAFFIO.

For obvious reasons. You see her husband is in the way here, and she can easily seek you in Venice.

GENNARO.

True, very true; it must be so. [*Crosses to* L.

MAFFIO (R.).

Come now, Gennaro! In pity's name, rouse up! Be either a child or a man; go to your nurse again, or join us at the table.

[MAFFIO *and* GENNARO *seat themselves at table.*

JEPPO (*down* L. C.).

Aha, Sir Truant, you have been found at last! Why, Maffio, where was he concealed? We thank you for executing your mission so faithfully, and bringing the poor wight before us. Ha, ha!

MAFFIO.

Come, Jeppo, give us a merry tale. The last time we met in Venice you gave us a serious story. Now give us its opposite, if you can.

PRINCESS (*coming forward*).

Signor Maffio [*he rises*], your friend seems not to participate in the general merriment. I trust he is not ill. He seems depressed and abstracted.

MAFFIO.

Madame, he is ever thus. You must pardon me for having brought him here without your invitation. He is my brother in arms, and we never separate. A Bohemian predicted that we should both die on the same day.

PRINCESS (*laughing*).

Did he say you would die in the morning or the evening?

MAFFIO.

In the morning, I think.

PRINCESS.

Then he knew nothing about it, I can tell you! So you love this young soldier?

MAFFIO.

Ay, madame, as much as one man *can* love another.

PRINCESS.

Then in friendship you must be happy.

MAFFIO.

Friendship does not occupy the entire heart, madame

PRINCESS.

Indeed, Count, what then?

MAFFIO.

Love, lady.

PRINCESS.

Ah, Count, you always have love on your lips.

MAFFIO.

And you in your eyes, dear lady.   [*Kissing her hand*

PRINCESS.

You are a bold man, Count Orsini.

MAFFIO.

And you — you are a charming woman, Princess
                             [*Puts his arm round her*

PRINCESS.

Count, release me! I shall be stifled, sir!

MAFFIO.

One kiss of this fair hand!

PRINCESS.

No, no!   [*She escapes from him; goes to her seat again.*

GUBETTA (*coming forward*, R.).

You seem in a fine train with the Princess.

MAFFIO. (L.).

And yet she always tell me "No."

GUBETTA.

Well, "no" on a woman's lips is the twin brother to "yes."

JEPPO (*comes forward*, L.).

Well, how do you get on? How do you find the Princess?

MAFFIO (C.).

Adorable!

JEPPO.

And her supper?

MAFFIO.

A feast for the gods! By the way, the Princess is a widow.

JEPPO.

I should have known that by her gaiety. Count Belverana, you'd hardly believe that Maffio was almost afraid to come here to-night.

GUBETTA (*crossing to* C.).

Afraid, was he? And of what?

JEPPO.

Of poison! and all because the palace of the Negroni touches the palace of the Borgia.

GUBETTA.

Devil take the Borgias! Let us drink, and think of them no more. [*Crosses behind to table*, L.

JEPPO (*low to* MAFFIO).

I like the Count for one thing, — he hates the Borgias.

MAFFIO.

Yes, he never lets a chance escape of sending them to the devil, without grace; and yet, Jeppo, I have observed that this Spaniard to-night has drunk nothing but water.

JEPPO.

Suspicious again!

GUBETTA (*coming forward*, L.).

Do you know, Signor Maffio, you resemble my grandfather, named Gil-Basieo Fernan-Ireno Filipe Frasco Frasqueto, Count of Belverana?

JEPPO (*low, to* MAFFIO, R.).

I hope and trust you'll never doubt his Spanish origin after that! [*Aloud.*] A good name, that of yours, Count; I hope you keep 'em catalogued!

GUBETTA.

My name was all my father had to give, and he gave me plenty of that. [*They laugh, and go up to table,* R. *Aside.*] I must try some way to get the ladies from the room, or I can never go to work. I have it! Signor Oloferno is drunk; I'll draw him into a quarrel: that'll do it. [*Goes to table,* R. H.

OLOFERNO (*partially drunk*).

Ladies, taste this wine! It is sweeter than the wine of Lachryma Christi, and more ardent than the wine of Cyprus. Drink; it is the wine of Syracuse, gentlemen!

GUBETTA.

It is evident that our friend is tipsy.

OLOFERNO.

Ladies, I will recite you some verses I have composed for this occasion. I wish I were a better poet; I would raise myself to heaven. I wish I had two wings.

GUBETTA.

Of the pheasant on my plate. Devil take your verses! More wine!

ALL.

More wine!

OLOFERNO.

Oh, you're no poet! Silence, for my song!

GUBETTA.

Spare us, Marquis of Oloferno. We beg leave to drink to your departed reason. I dispense you from your song.

OLOFERNO.

You dispense me from my song! You dispense!

GUBETTA.

Ay, as I would dispense a barking dog, or the devil from blessing me.

OLOFERNO.

You mean to insult me, Sir *Spaniard!*

GUBETTA.

I merely decline listening to your song, Signor *Italian!* I had rather taste the Cyprus wine in my throat than have your song in my ears.

OLOFERNO.

Your ears, you miserable Castilian refugee! I'll shave them off close to your dog's head!

GUBETTA.

You are an absurd and ridiculous dunce! Didst ever see the like? He gets drunk with Syracuse wine, and has the demeanour of a man intoxicated with beer. I can't stop to carve such poultry as you now; it is too troublesome.

OLOFERNO.

I'll carve you to pieces!

GUBETTA.

As I do this pheasant now. Ladies, shall I help you?

OLOFERNO (*seizing a knife*).

By the Virgin! I'd stab the miscreant, were he in a church.

[*The Lords and Ladies rise in alarm, and exclaiming, "They are going to fight!" rush out of the room* R. *and* L. *The friends hold* OLOFERNO, *and disarm him.*

OLOFERNO.

Set me free!

GUBETTA.

My worthy friend, your poetry has put the ladies to flight. On my word, you are a gay troubadour, Signor Vitellozzo!

JEPPO.

The ladies have gone indeed!

MAFFIO.

Let a knife glitter, and a woman flies

OLOFERNO.

Count, keep your valour warm till morning, and I'll meet you then.

GUBETTA.

If you do, I'm your man! Ha, ha, ha! You have put to flight the fairest ladies of Ferrara with a carving-knife and a song. You should have wings, for in truth you are a perfect goose of a man.

JEPPO.

Come, cease this quarrel. It is enough that we have lost the ladies. Cut one another's throats in the morning at your leisure, and fight like gentlemen, with swords, and not like cooks, with carving-knives.

ASCANIO.

Apropos! where are our swords?

APOSTOLO.

You forget they obliged us to leave them in the anteroom, as we came in.

GENNARO (*who has not moved*).

It was a wise precaution, too, it seems.

MAFFIO.

Egad, brother Gennaro, that is the first thing you have uttered to-night. And you have not drunk. You are dreaming of the fair Lucretia; do not deny it.

GENNARO.

No more of that, Maffio! Come, fill me to drink. I'll meet my friend with good wine with the same courage as I would a foe in the field with weapons of death.

MAFFIO.

Fill me with the wine of Syracuse!

ALL.

The wine of Syracuse!

JEPPO.

A pest on all brawls. The ladies have gone, and will not return, it seems. [*Tries all the doors.*] And every door is fastened on the other side, too!

GUBETTA.

Rather a wise movement, I think, from past experience. Come, the wine!

[*Enter* ASTOLFO, 1 E., L. H., *with salver, one bottle of wine, and seven glasses.*

GENNARO.

Gentlemen, let us drink.

MAFFIO.

Ay, to the health, long life, and happiness of Gennaro; and may you soon find your mother.

GENNARO.

May Heaven grant it!

[*All drink, except* GUBETTA, *who throws his wine over his shoulder.*

MAFFIO (*aside, to* JEPPO).

Ha! did you see that?

JEPPO.

See what?

MAFFIO.

The Spaniard did not drink.

JEPPO.

Well.

MAFFIO.

He has thrown it over his shoulder!

JEPPO.

Pooh! the Count is drunk, and so are you, I think.

MAFFIO (*carelessly*).

Very like, very like!

GUBETTA (*aside*).

I must feign to be drunk. [*Aloud.*] A drinking-song, gentlemen! I will give you a bacchanalian song worth more than the love sonnet of our amiable friend, the Marquis of Oloferno. But first let me swear, by the old skull of my old father, that this same song is none of my making. I'm not a poet, and never could jingle two lines into rhyme in any way. So here goes. It is addressed to Monsieur Saint Peter, the famous doorkeeper of paradise, — a jolly lover of wine, like ourselves.

JEPPO.

He's drunk as Bacchus! He's more than drunk; he's a drunkard!

ALL (*except* GENNARO).

The song! the song!

GUBETTA (*rising and reeling*).

"Saint Peter, I pray you, quick open your gates,
   And let in some topers you know;
With voice full and strong, and thick fuddled pates,
   In chorus to chant 'Domino'!"

ALL (*except* GENNARO).

Gloria Domino!

[*General laughing, clinking of glasses, etc.; cries of "Bravo!" Amid the uproar, distant voices are heard without, chanting in a slow and solemn strain from the Roman ritual.*

CHORUS OF MONKS.

"De profundis clamavi ad te, Domine! Conquassibat capita in terra multorum!" [*Lights gradually down.*

JEPPO (*roaring with laughter*).

Do you hear that? By the rubicund visage of jolly old Bacchus, while we sing bacchanalian songs, echo chants the vespers! A full church chorus!

MAFFIO.

Some procession is passing, I think.

GENNARO (*who is seated in* L., *apart from the others*).

A procession at midnight! No, no; that is rather too late!

JEPPO.

Oh, nonsense! On with your song, Count!

ALL.

Ay! the song, the song!
[*Beat table.* GUBETTA *rises, reeling.*

MONKS (*chant without, nearer*).

"De profundis clamavi ad te, Domine! Conquassibat capita in terra multorum!"
[*All the cavaliers laugh again vociferously*

JEPPO.

How these monks bellow! They are regular night brawlers! [*Lights half down.*

ASCANIO.

Ay, but they are kicking up a riot in the streets; we in doors! [*Lights down.*

MAFFIO.

Halloa! the lamps are going out! We shall be in the dark presently!

GENNARO.

They seemed to be near at hand, and I think it is the service for the dead.

MAFFIO.

Very likely, very likely.

JEPPO.

Let us drink to the poor defunct, — poor devil!

GUBETTA (*meaningly*).

I shouldn't wonder if it were for four or five, instead of one.

JEPPO.

Well, more or less, here's to all their healths, and a safe journey through purgatory. [*All laugh.*] Go on, Count, with your song, — your invocation to Saint Peter.

GUBETTA.

Speak civilly of Monsieur Saint Peter, the grand usher and patent turnkey of paradise. We may need his good offices soon.

ALL.

The song! the song!

GUBETTA.

"To the songster so joyous, glass filled to the brim,
　And belly so large, ripe for fun,
When he enters your portals, at first glimpse of him,
　You would swear it a butt or a tun!"

ALL.

Gloria Domino!

[*Chant: solemn music. All touch glasses, with peals of laughter, which is continued, while the large curtains slowly open, discovering a large hall hung with black. A large altar in* C., *lighted, covered with black, with a large silver crucifix in* C. *of it. Six monks slowly enter, in cowl and scapulars of black, with their faces all concealed, except by the apertures of their vizards, for them to see through. Each bears a torch; and as they range down stage on* R., *they chant in a loud and solemn tone.*

MONKS.

"De profundis clamavi ad te, Domine! Conquassibat," etc.

[*All the cavaliers stare with astonishment at them and each other.*

MAFFIO.

What — what does this mean!

JEPPO (*laughing*).

Ha, ha, ha! a capital joke! I see it now! These are our charming countesses, disguised thus to try our courage. If we raise their masks we shall find them the visages of mischievous, laughing, and beautiful women. Just see!

[*He lifts the mask of one of the monks, and it reveals the pale and ghastly countenance of an aged man, calm, silent, motionless.* JEPPO *and others stand horror-struck.*

MAFFIO.

Great heavens! what means this? My blood congeals with horror round my heart!

JEPPO.

This is too awful! We are ensnared! Our swords! our swords!

MAFFIO.

Quick, or we are lost! This is the house of fiends!

[LUCRETIA, *dressed in black, appears at* C. D

LUCRETIA.

Yes, you are in my palace!
[*Close curtains, and lights up gradually.*

ALL (*except* GENNARO, *who is unseen, on* L. H.).
Lucretia Borgia!

LUCRETIA.

Ay, Lucretia Borgia! [*She slowly advances, with a sarcastic smile, and gazes on them.*] Yes, gallant Venetians you are the guests of the Duchess of Ferrara,—of Lucretia Borgia! There was a time—I have not forgotten it—when in Venice you spoke that name with scorn, contempt, and withering hatred; now it comes from the trembling lips of terror. Look on me, and listen. When last we met, my heart was softened, my feelings changed, my nature humanized, and sorrow and repentance for the past had bowed me to the earth. I had resolved never more to terrify Italy with frightful deeds. One feeling of nature still filled my bosom; it was love,—a pure and holy love for one whose fate for years I had in secret and in silence watched. You met me before him, and your eyes feasted on my wretchedness with exultation and triumph. You scorned my anguish, you mocked my sufferings, laughed at my misery, insulted my despair, tore from my face the mask, while my supplications for mercy were met with shouts of derision, and every epithet of ignominy and shame heaped upon my head. I could have borne all, had you not spoken it before him! It was but that I begged for; but you were merciless! I rose from that spot with the spirit of a demon in my heart; I swore to have revenge,—awful and fearful revenge. I have kept my oath! Ay, look at me once more! You are all poisoned! Ha. ha. ha!

ALL.

Poisoned!

LUCRETIA.

Ay, do not stir; the room without is full of armed men, and, my good friends, your deaths are sealed beyond the power of fate itself to change. Now, hear me; it is my turn. I think I have returned your civilities to me. You entertained me at a ball in Venice, I you with a supper at Ferrara, — *féte* for *féte*, feast for feast!

JEPPO.

This is a horrible waking from a wild dream of mirth!

MAFFIO.

Ay, my friend. We are dying! I feel it even now; but let us meet death unshrinkingly, and like men!

LUCRETIA.

Remember me at the carnival of Venice, and tell me, have I not, for a woman, well avenged myself for all the agony you then forced me to endure? Do you understand the word "vengeance" now? Holy fathers, conduct these men into the adjoining room, and shrive them; and do it quickly, for their time is short! For you, sirs, fear not; these are real monks of St. Sixtus; and I will also comfort you with the assurance that, while I thought of your souls, I have not neglected your bodies. [*Stamps.*] Open! Behold! [*Music, ending with chord. Curtains open, and ranged round the altar are five coffins, covered with black, on which are painted, in large white letters, the names of the five cavaliers. All start with horror.*] The exact number, — five! Maffio, Jeppo, Oloferno, Ascanio, and Apostolo, — exactly five!

GENNARO (*coming forward*).

And mine, madame, — where is the sixth?

LUCRETIA (*starting back*).

Powers of mercy! Gennaro!

GENNARO.

Yes, I am Gennaro.

LUCRETIA.

I *am* accursed and helpless! [*Sees* GUBETTA *on* R.]. Traitor! villain! accursed fiend! Did I not bid thee shield him as thine own eye?

GUBETTA.

I knew not thy motive; thy secret was too great for me, and he drank what I prepared, with the others, — his potion the same.

LUCRETIA (*stabbing him*).

And this be thine, thrice damned villain!

GUBETTA.

I die, but he dies also, mistress! I — oh — [*Dies.*

LUCRETIA.

Cast that carrion into the streets! [*The body is carried off,* R., *by the Guards.*] Monks, accompany your charges to the altar! All, all leave me, except Gennaro; and whatever may be heard or conjectured of what passes here, let no one dare to enter! Begone!

[*She sinks into a chair,* R. *Solemn music is heard behind. Monks go off,* C., *each with a cavalier chanting,* " De profundis clamavi ad te, Domine!" *etc. Curtains close.* LUCRETIA *comes down* R., *and gazes a moment with agony on* GENNARO, *who returns it sternly.*

LUCRETIA.

Oh, Gennaro!

GENNARO.

Well, madame.

LUCRETIA.

Gennaro! Gennaro! how do I find you here, when I thought you leagues away? By what strange fatality does every blow from my hand fall on thy devoted head? Father of mercy! why are you here?

GENNARO.

It is my destiny.

LUCRETIA.

Gennaro! Oh, my God! Gennaro, you are dying,— again poisoned!

GENNARO.

Well, madame. And yet I still have your gift,— *this!*

LUCRETIA (*with a scream of joy*).

Thank Heaven! The antidote! You are saved! Drink!

GENNARO.

One word first: is there enough in this phial to save my friends?

LUCRETIA (*examines it*).

Barely enough for thee, Gennaro! Oh, quick! take it!

GENNARO.

Can you obtain more in time to save them?

LUCRETIA.

All that I possessed you have. Ere I could get more, it would be too late.

GENNARO.

It is very well. [*Putting phial into his bosom.*

LUCRETIA (*alarmed*).

What is well? Nothing can be well till you have taken that. I implore you, do not play with your life! Trifle not now: a few moments longer, and it will be too late. Quick! you can yet escape, and ere the dawn be far from Ferrara! I will furnish the means. Drink that antidote, and let us part! Oh, you *must*, you *shall* take it, and *live*, Gennaro, *live!*

GENNARO (*seizing knife from table, and speaking sternly*).

And you, madame, must die!

LUCRETIA (*incredulously*).

How? What say you, Gennaro?

GENNARO.

You have, through your hellish agent, infamously, treacherously, poisoned five men, my dear friends, — men of rank and name; and among them Maffio Orsini, my brother in heart, my companion in arms, he who twice saved my life in battle; and between us all, vengeance is common. I am his and their avenger! You must die!

LUCRETIA.

Die! and by your hand, Gennaro? No; that is impossible! It cannot be!

GENNARO.

It *will* be, madame, and quickly, too, for I am dying also; I feel it here! So, while I address my prayers on high for mercy, do you the same, with clasped hands and bended knees, before that God you have so terribly outraged!

LUCRETIA.

This is some awful dream! *Thou* take *my* life? It is too fearful! No, no; I'll not believe it! I say again, it is impossible! Amid my most frightful conceptions, *that* is the most agonizing that ever swept across my brain! No, no; He who knows all will not permit it!

[*Crosses to* L. H.

GENNARO (*seizing her arm*).

My throbbing brain and beating heart cry out for haste; I must obey their voice! [*Raises his arm.*

LUCRETIA (*winding about him, and falling before him on her knees*).

Gennaro, cast aside that knife, as you hope for Heaven's mercy! [*He raises knife.*] Hold, oh, hold, one moment, and listen to me! Did you but know all! But cast that knife aside; I cannot speak while that flashes in my sight! Stay! know you who I am or who you are? The time has come when you must know all. The same blood flows in our veins, Gennaro! you are a Borgia, son of the Duke of Candia, and I —

GENNARO.

I, then, am a Borgia! — nephew of Lucretia Borgia! Oh, horror! My mother, then, was the Duchess of Candia, she whom the Borgias have made wretched! It is you of whom my poor mother spoke in her letters as the cause of her unhappiness! It is you who murdered my father, and drowned in tears and blood the hopes of a wife and mother! I am a Borgia! The thought will drive me mad! Hear me! I have a mother's wrongs to avenge, and on you, my aunt! Your life has been blackened by so many crimes, it must be hateful to you! I will rid you of its heavy burden! I, Lucretia Borgia, am to slay you; therefore commend your soul to God, for your fate is sealed!

LUCRETIA.

Gennaro, Gennaro! you are as yet innocent of crime! Oh, have mercy! Your hands are yet free from innocent blood, your heart yet unclogged by crime; oh, keep it so! I entreat you, commit not this murder!

GENNARO.

Murder! crime! My head wanders, my sight darkens! Is it with the thought of crime? No, no; am I not a Borgia? My heritage is murder! shall I disgrace my name by mercy to another? No!

LUCRETIA.

I will call for help.

GENNARO.

Do so! No one will answer! You yourself forbade it; and if they did, ere they could reach you it would be too late.

LUCRETIA.

Gennaro, would you assassinate a woman, — a helpless woman, — and you a soldier? You have a soul too noble for so vile a deed! You call me vile, criminal, wicked; if I am, cut me not off thus; or, if I must die, it cannot, must not be by your hand!

GENNARO.

I will not, dare not hear more. Are you not my aunt? Lucretia Borgia, where, where is my mother?

LUCRETIA.

Oh, my heart! I cannot tell him all. Spare my life! I will submit to any infliction! Shall I hie to a cloister? Say you so, I'll do it. Yes, to obey you, I'll look for the last time on the bright world; for you my head shall be shorn, my bed ashes, my raiment sackcloth, while my bare feet shall tread the flinty floor of my cell, and my hours shall be passed in prayers for forgiveness of Heaven for past sins, and for blessings upon you. Gennaro, hear me. [*He seems faint.*] Ah, you turn pale! Why have we wasted the precious moments? Quick! drink that antidote! It is not yet too late; save your own life — spare mine! Do not, I beg, implore you, perpetuate crime to your name, and by such a deed as will forever blast your peace while living and your memory when dead! Speak! let me hear your voice! and do not, do not kill an unhappy woman, who kneels and supplicates for mercy!

GENNARO (*moved and softened*).

Madame! [*Drops knife.*

LUCRETIA.

Ah, you relent! your eyes fill with tears, your hand trembles in mine; you will not, cannot slay me!

MAFFIO (*within*, C.).

Gennaro!

GENNARO (*starting*).

Ah! what voice is that? Who is it calls me?

MAFFIO.

It is I — Maffio — your brother! I die, Gennaro! Avenge me!

GENNARO.

Avenge thee, my brother? I will, I will! Lucretia Borgia, you've heard your doom! A voice cries from the grave, "Revenge!" Hark! You must die! [*Raises knife.*

LUCRETIA (*struggling*).

Mercy! One word more!

GENNARO.

No! it is too late!

LUCRETIA.

Oh, spare me! spare me!

GENNARO.

No!

LUCRETIA.

In the name of Heaven!

GENNARO.

Fate decrees it! Die! [*Stabs her.*

LUCRETIA.

Gennaro, you have killed me! I AM YOUR MOTHER!

GENNARO (*with a scream of despair*).

O God! my mother! [*He falls dead before her.*

LUCRETIA.

Gennaro! dear Gennaro! My son, I do forgive thee! It may not be too late yet! the phial! [*Crawls to his body. She takes the phial, puts it to his lips, then exclaims.*] Dead! [*Kisses him. Monks within chant, "De profundis," etc.*] Gennaro! [*Dies.*]

THE END.

www.ingramcontent.com/pod-product-compliance
Lightning Source LLC
Chambersburg PA
CBHW011950150426
43195CB00018B/2884